D1190344

Ancient Egypt and Secrets of the Sun

by Jerry Parker

Ancient Egypt and Secrets of the Sun

by Jerry Parker

Photos by Jerry Parker

Book Design by Brad Samuels, Samuels Design Inc.

Copyright 1994, May 1995 by Golden Obelisk Press, Inc.

Jerry Parker
P.O. BOX 377640
Chicago, IL. 60637-7940

All rights reserved. No part of this book may be reproduced in any form or by any means without permission in writing from publisher.

Library of Congress
Catalog Card Number 073629689
ISBN: 978-0-9637021-1-1
Printed in the United States of America

ABOUT THE BOOK COVER

The Eye of Horus is one of the most powerful and respected principle of the Ancient Egyptians. It represents the physical light and the mental insight that the Ancient Egyptians were endowed with by the Sun. The front cover of this book displays a powerful depiction of the Great Pyramid of Egypt (The Pyramid of the Sun), This pyramid is highlighted by the Eye of Horus, station over it as an annular solar eclipse, incorporating the sun as the iris and the moon as the pupil of its eye, as it casts light knowledge and intellect over Egypt.

The back cover feathers the first gigantic stone structure engineered and built in ancient times, The Step Pyramid of Saqqara Egypt. Right below, the author appears in a picture with the funeral Mask of Tutankhamun taken in 1992, at the Museum of Antiquity.

ANCIENT EGYPT AND THE SECRETS OF THE SUN

CONTENTS

Acknowledgements & Dedication

I dedicate this book to my entire family, especially to my sons Davion and Jerry, my assistants and constant weekend companions who have demonstrated a strong interest in our people's condition and a willingness to continue this work.

This book is also dedicated to Sojourner Truth and Paul Robeson for putting their people before their personal interests, careers and welfare. To Harriet Tubman, Malcolm X and Dr. Martin Luther King for putting their people before their families and lives. To every African activist and author who have made sincere attempts to lift the consciousness of our people.

To Arnetta May Williams for her encouragement, assistance and early interest in this offering. To Walter Williams, my mentor from 1985 to 1997, who casted a large sphere of influence and respect for his powerful life's work. In addition, I would like to dedicate this book to Louis Bobo and Daniel Lee who share with me the vision and scope of this project. They are my fellow brothers who have made my calling their calling in bringing this book forward.

INTRODUCTION
BY LOUIS BOBO

Brother Jerry Parker is challenging some concepts sanctioned by a faction of the academic community that has in effect made White Supremacy a religion. He brings clarity to that which is hidden behind the illusion of reality and gives us the understanding that the source of all knowledge emanates from the creator as manifested in nature. And that with this compass we can find our way back to our true selves. And just as surely as we are all victimized by perverted scholarship we are all beneficiaries of excellence in the promulgation of truth.

Although he has undertaken the awesome task of setting the record straight, even when it flies in the face of what passes for the truth, he has the necessary credentials to do the work by his application of the Maatian creed principle. To the extent that alienation from the truth is alienation from ones self, when we are aligned with the truth we are free even when our physical surroundings suggest our enslavement.

Brother Parker delineates the fundamental principle derived from the observation of the interaction of the Sun, Moon and the Earth that the Ancient Egyptian applied in developing the civilization that gave light to the world. But unfortunately a measure of psychopathology is the obsession to steal that which has been given. And though we find ourselves in the belly of this unlikely beast, we are instructed to hold fast to Ma at to preclude worshipping the beast as God.

To my mentor and brother on the occasion of his sacred gift to the world I offer this prayer:

Oh ancient ancestral gods of our fathers manifest in our deliverance from the belly of the great white whale of meaninglessness which has devoured generations of unsuspecting black souls too caught up on the treadmill of worshipping our oppressor to turnaround in ourselves and call on the gods of our father. Manifest in our deliverance into the humane community of Genuine African brotherhood of the New Man. For we would sing the song - dance the rhythm - walk the way of true sons and daughters of mother Africa. All praise is due the ancestors, all praise is due Amen Ra.

Louis Bobo

Words from the Author

The foremost sign of an oppressed people can be seen in their inability to see or define their existence outside the domain of their oppressor. Yet, people of African origin constantly confine themselves to Western standards, as if these standards are the ultimate manifestation of consciousness.

Fresh, adventurous, bold, innovative, and new research are adjectives that do not have a place in today's historical scholarship. Nevertheless, these are the claims given to many of the writers today. If one is to be a historian or a serious student of history, it is not enough to report on history, nor is it enough to analyze a historical concept on the surface. Critical analysis is essential, particularly for the African scholar. Western academia must be challenged down to its foundation.

Nothing should be taken for granted. Yet the majority of Western doctrines and philosophies are given a pass. The purpose of this examination is not to critique a particular author or work, but to expose a movement that is responsible for so many of our African authors and educators becoming an unintentional party to Western deception.

To characterize the traditional relationship between African Scholars and Western academia as similar to that of a parent and child relationship would be a gross overstatement. Primarily because the dominate member of this association (Western Academia) does not have the best interests of the dependent member (African scholars) at heart. A master/ servant designation would be more accurate.

There is a reason why it took Dr. Walter Williams to usher in a new era of reasoning. I am not suggesting that it is impossible for someone who has been bestowed the highest degree of Western academia to come up with creative thinking, divorced and devoid of Western influences. I am suggesting, however, that it is highly unlikely under the current dictates of historical research and investigation.

Although, there are hundreds of African Scholars who are an exception to this rule as partially illustrated by the bibliography of this book, for the most part African Scholars, or any scholars, who are trained by Western institutions have not and will not deviate significantly from their Western training. Our African Scholars must be conscious of the fact that the institution on which they rely to validate them is the same entity that limits and restrains their thinking. If African Scholars invalidate Western philosophy, they also invalidate their own credibility, the very thing that separates and holds them apart as an authority. The Western educational system must be thought of as a filtering system, which takes an individual through a series of indoctrinating processes until the individual emerges as the polished product of Western world interest regardless of race or nationality.

A PH.D. Is the highest degree Western academia confers on an individual. It is equivalent to a Doctor of Philosophy. Doctor is synonymous with teacher. Therefore, Ph.D. ultimately means teacher or master of Western philosophy. Subsequently, it stands to reason that even people of African origin will forcefully uphold Western philosophy. Following years of indoctrination this philosophy in most instances has become the foundation of their makeup and thinking.

Since the dogma promoted by Western educational institutions is politically motivated and psychologically formulated, a scholastic system based on previous documentation must be deemphasized. Documentation must be down played while critical analysis must be encouraged, promoted and highlighted at every turn. We must make a way for higher knowledge because it is mentally liberating. Far too many of our scholars have joined a conspiracy of silence. This is particularly the case when the bearer of this knowledge has been certified by Western academia and the individual is wearing the badge and emblems of Western philosophy.

The primary purpose of this work is to expose Western institutions down to their core. Thereby, revealing a multi-layer of superficial philosophies, theologies, theories, and incarnated characters used to hide the greatness of the Ancient Egyptians and their solar principles. The Sun governs and regulates the environment on Earth and it serves as the true foundation of a higher civilization. These principles have been altered and perverted by Western institutions.

If we are to be masters of our own fate we can no longer allow European scholars and Western institutions to be the ultimate arbiter of what is right, or wrong, what is true or false, what is important or trivial. We must take control of our own destiny by reclaiming our true history in order to determine our future.

The concept of a chosen people is a prominent theme in Western culture. However, realistically and historically this concept can only be applied to the people who brought civilization to the world. The people of the African continent. The Ancient Egyptians. Africa is the only continent that is symmetrically divided by the equator. Its original inhabitants wear the honor of having dark or tanned skin (the kiss of the Sun). The terms Children of the Sun, people of the Sun and descendants of the Sun, all take on a very powerful connotation especially when one understands the powerful linkage between the African continent, the Sun, and the Ancient Egyptians. The Sun and the Earth's orbit of the Sun having a strong influence in their culture will then reveal itself as the blueprint for their high civilization.

It has been stated, the reason Europeans have dominated the world so completely, is because they have colonized most of the collective knowledge of the world. It has also been stated that if people of African origin are to control their own destiny, the European Scholarly community must be forced to relinquish their stranglehold on this body of knowledge. However, it is my contention that the European domination of the world is not due to their ability to control the dissemination of key information, but rather is due to their ability to control not only how one thinks, but what one thinks.

Western religious and educational institutions are the primary tools in this endeavor. The mass media is the secondary facilitator. One must always understand that the European elite do not make laws for themselves. They are in practice above the law. Western laws are made to limit the thinking and action of non-Europeans. Therefore, the European community has dictated to the world their philosophy and values thus becoming masters of psychology, hence they are able to systematically impose powerful paradigms through their institutions. This allows them to disseminate lies and theories in the form of empirical data. Thereby, creating an illusion of them as the ultimate authority and making it unthinkable for most people to think outside of the parameters that their Western institutions have established.

However, one of the profound defects in the European psyche has proven to be their inability to see related phenomenon as one integrated whole, rather than as independent occurrence. Analytically, one of the most crucial elements of problem solving lies in the ability to break a situation down to its lowest relevant level, and to understand the mechanics of the situation at that level. Then reassemble the situation as one collective whole. This approach is known as a holistic view, however, this is one of the many crucial areas, where the European psyche has failed them. We must reacclimatize ourselves to the fact that historically, in native cultures throughout the world, the various components, that made up these societies were not departmentalized. Education, spirituality and government were so intertwined in these societies that they were inseparable.

However, the uniqueness of the European mind set is that they are able to put aside any component of a whole to go after their objectives. The result of this is that all of their pre-imposed principles or rules are discarded. This is the same vein that allows people of European descent to beat or lynch a person of African origin without a second thought. Freshly out of church service, shortly after proclaiming the virtue of peace, love and brotherhood.

We must acclimate ourselves to the fact that the current political philosophy of one world order, is actually the second coming of this idea, this time under an economic banner submerged in capitalism. This idea was originally manifested in a religious motif through Catholicism (which means universal) centuries earlier.

Because Egypt is within the continent of Africa, and the people of Ancient Egypt and the indigenous people of Africa are racially one, the intent of this book is to present the reader with a holistic view on people of African origin.

Book I: Book of the Moon
Western Philosophy: Facts or Theories and Lies

Book I discusses the protocol of Western domination. In part, this protocol consists of introducing an idea as a theory, then, postulating that idea as a fact, subsequently introducing additional theories, based on the original theory, then advancing these theories as facts. This amounts to building lies on top of lies. While passing off theories and lies as real science and true history.

Book II: Book of the Earth
Africa and Africans Misunderstood

Book II discusses the cultural and social contribution of the continent of Africa. This book also dispels precepts, lies and myths that are falsely assigned to Sub Sahara Africa and Africans, and squarely roots Sub Saharan Africa to highly developed social systems while revealing Sub Saharan Africas irrevocable link to the contributions given exclusively to Northern Africa.

Book III: The Book of the Sun
Ancient Egypt = The Sun (RA), Time,
Spirituality and Civilization

Book III reveals the true relationship between the Ancient Egyptian Spiritual system and the formation of a time concept and the establishment of the world's first civilization. This time concept serves as the catalyst and foundation for the development of the world's major religious, political and educational institutions.

The objective of this dissertation is to bring some truth to what is generally accepted as conventional thought and education (Western philosophy). Primarily by dismissing the imposter of Ancient civilization, the Greeks, while fostering the Ancient Egyptians and their descendants as the legitimate creator of high civilization. Secondly, to expose the general meaning behind Western institutions and specifically, to reveal for the first time the secret meaning of Western religions.

Jerry Parker,
Analyst, Naturalist and Free Thinker

BOOK I
THE BOOK OF THE MOON

WESTERN PHILOSOPHY:
FACTS OR THEORIES AND LIES

Book I Outline

The Western World is waging a psychological assault on the minds of people throughout the world. This attack is designed to dismiss their critics through name calling and labeling. This technique is also designed to divert attention from indictments by assailing their critics. The Western media has effectively neutralized the critics of the west by labeling them radical, extremist, leftist, right wing, or liberal. Desperate, radical, or extreme problems in some instances require radical or extreme solutions. To label an individual or group does not address the charges. However, it does suggest that the charges cannot be satisfactorily answered.

The Theory of the Evolution of Man

In Western academia, the deception is constantly building and the lies are multiplying. This is accomplished primarily by creating a theory and then postulating that theory as a fact.

Case in point, the theories of the origin of man. In the Western world view there are basically two recognized theories pertaining to the origin of man, the Adam and Eve, or creation theory, and the theory of evolution, or Darwinism. The Adam and Eve theory is the product of biblical literature and the theory of evolution is the outcome of the Western scientific community. The Adam and Eve theory is totally rejected by the academic community and the theory of evolution is totally rejected by the Western religious community. Both theories are completely groundless. However, because Western academia validates the theory of evolution, this theory will be the subject of our examination.

I am among the first to agree that the natural order of things is to evolve from small to large and from the simple to the complex. The theory of evolution establishes its base in Africa. Africa is the only continent where you find the Great Apes, animals which have anatomical characteristics similar to humans. This theory states that man evolved from the apes of Africa, thereby producing the first man in Africa. Before man is produced the ape starts off in a primitive state, then progresses through a series of evolutionary phases and migrates from Africa to China evolving into the Peking man. From China he then goes to Europe developing into the Neanderthal man, changing from a primate to a human. The people who put this theory together used an unbelievable amount of inference. In most cases only a skull fragment was the only tangible evidence, but this still did not stop the theorists from claiming success in determining the specimen's sex, age, health, and appearance. At each phase it is theorized that these apes take on a human-like appearance as their bodies continue to stand more erect. However, Western scholars believe that there is an evolutionary phase that has yet to be discovered, a "missing link." This phase in their minds would complete the evolutionary process. The theory takes on a very believable air especially when the whole Western academic community gives it validation. However, if one is an independent thinker, this theory becomes just another psychological ploy of Western academia.

Embedded within this same theory is its politically loaded companion, "Survival of the Fittest." This theory is deceptively introduced at a non-human level. It simply states that those animals that survive for longer periods of time deserve to survive because they adapt to their environment. Conversely, those animals that perished did so because they could not adapt to their environment. These theories were created in an era that sought to bring justification for the West African slave trade, European imperialism, white supremacy, and the European physical colonization of the most of the world.

The problem with the theory of evolution of man is that in the real world, mutation occurs. A biological unit can evolve and take on additional characteristics that it previously did not have and a unit can drop characteristics that it formerly had. However, there is a limit to this principle. Mutations that occur within specie stay within that specie. There is no transformation from one specie to another. If humans evolved from apes and if the theory of evolution were correct, that process would be at work this very moment. For evolution is not a one time phenomenon, it is an ongoing process. We would be able to witness animals going through evolutionary phases firsthand. We would be able to see and verify that process today. Another point of contention is, if this theory were true there would be no one cell animals, no monkey, no gorilla, no chimpanzee, or any other lower animal life form. They all would have evolved to their highest state. As you can see this is not the reality of the situation. The fact that one cell animals, monkeys, dogs, cats, snakes, and birds existed millions of years ago and still exist today destroys that theory completely. If that theory were correct they would have evolved not only to a higher life form, but would be evolving to the highest manifestation of life. Rather, what we have today are animals characterized by their species and confined within their type. Lemurs are not evolving into monkeys, monkeys are not evolving into sloths, sloths are not evolving into chimpanzees, chimpanzees are not evolving into orangutans, orangutans are not evolving into gorillas, and gorillas are not evolving into European white men.

If the original man came out of Africa like what is universally believed, then what is deemed as man did not leave as one specie and then over hundreds of thousands of years evolve into another species. The original human came out of Africa as man, developed as man and is man today. Changes may have occurred to the original man over hundreds of thousands of years development, but not to the extent that the original human jumps from one specie to another specie or from ape to man. This can be said to be true of other species. Gorilla and chimpanzee were gorilla and chimpanzee hundreds of thousands of years ago. Gorilla and chimpanzee further developed into their species and today gorilla and chimpanzee are still gorilla and chimpanzee.

The Black Hole Theory

Another concept that was introduced as a theory, but now postulated as a fact is the concept known as a Black Hole. This theory defines a Black Hole as a collapsed dwarf star. This collapsed star is stated to have a gravitational force so powerful that nothing can escape its presence. Subsequently, within this vacuum, everything in it's path is devoured. This force is said to be so strong that not even the light of the star can escape its gravitational field, hence, the term Black Hole. This concept, as far as I know, has never been challenged in academic circles. Nevertheless, this does not make it right. We are aware that this theory has been accepted by Western academia, but let us determine whether it can stand the test of common sense and basic logic. Black Holes are said to be hundreds of light years away. A light year is the distance that light travels within a year which is approximately six trillion miles. Scientists are said to be able to detect Black Holes with radar telescopes. Many astronomers think that Black Holes make up as much as a third of the matter in the Earth's galaxy, the Milky Way. But how is it possible to detect a Black Hole with a radar telescope, given that the radar telescope has only been in existence for a few decades?

Consequently, these objects are supposed to be so far away that their signals have not had enough time to reach the Black Hole, notwithstanding a return. Then it is stated that the signals that are being received from these objects were emitted many years earlier. However, the point that should be especially noted is that theorizing about a Black Hole and proving the existence of a Black Hole poses a very critical contradiction. One cannot expect to prove their existence with a radar telescope simply because, hypothetically, even if they exist, radio signals (which are a type of electromagnetic wave or light wave which fall within certain frequencies) can only represent a vector. Theoretically, as soon as these signals approach the Black Hole it would be consumed by the Black Hole's gravitational field. These signals would never return.

Just because there is no air in space, does not suggest that space is void of other forces that could influence, redirect, and absorb those signals. Besides, if radio signals have limitations on Earth, then they certainly have limitations in space. A true vacuum is a theoretical condition that could never exist; for wherever one goes in the universe, there will be some type of force acting on any given body.

How is it possible to get a picture from a radio signal? The answer is by way of a process and a device to interrupt the signals, the new process of computer aided imaging. A computer is a device that can make a multitude of calculations and comparisons in a short period of time. A computer, however is completely dependent on the programmer that sets its standards, parameters, and conditions.

Computers and the Internet: The New Authority

Western institutions have conditioned the world into believing that computers are infallible and anything emanating from them should not be questioned. The people and institutions who fill the textbooks, magazines, newspapers, radio, television, and movies with false and fictional information are the same people who are supplying these computers with their database and program logic. However, there are times when data or program logic can be unintentionally falsified. In either case, the end result is corrupted. On the other hand, a desired result can be induced at any point, making it hard to detect by a layman.

There is nothing absolute or sacred about a programmer or computer, so the conclusions that any computer derives, can come from the calculated intent of the programmer. Currently there is a movement in this country to confine all reference information regarding any subject to the computer. What this will do is reduce by tenfold the number of people who are responsible for defining our world. Ultimately, coming up with only one world perception.

Absolute Zero

The concept of absolute zero is yet another theory that is postulated and introduced as fact. The temperature for absolute zero is said to be (-273.15° C) or (-459.67° F). This is claimed to be the point where the subatomic or atomic movement stops. If you can establish a limit to how cold an object can get, you can establish a limit to how hot an object can get. You can also impose how small an object can be or how large the universe is. Let me suggest that it is impossible for man to impose or prove the limits of any natural phenomenon. How can a temperature reach into the millions of degrees, but a temperature can not get any colder than (-273.15 °C). The Sun is said to be millions of degrees hot at it's center. How can that be factually verified? What instrument can be used to prove these conjectures.

The Change in Seasons

It is interesting to note that Western scientists make all kinds of outlandish claims and projections concerning deep space, from the birth of a star to the formation of galaxies. Yet, it is fascinating to point out that these same authorities can not effectively explain the dynamics between the Sun and the Earth which supposedly causes the change of seasons on Earth.

Winter, Spring, Summer, and Fall.

The theory that is projected as a fact is based on the premise that the Earth rotates around the Sun with it's North/South axis on a 23½ degree angle, thereby causing the seasons to change. The problem with this premise is that only the summer and winter solstice can be graphically illustrated. What can not be illustrated is the vernal and autumnal equinox, the transition from the summer solstice to the autumnal equinox, and the transition from the winter solstice to the vernal equinox. This not only suggests, but dictates that this principle, in reality, is not only a theory, but a poor one at that. The European scholars have set themselves up as the ultimate authority and as an all knowing pseudo god. Yet there is no one who is challenging these illusions. No one has ever seen an atom or molecule, yet the periodic chart of elements claims to predict the atomic weight and composition of various elements. Western scientists claim to alter genes. Yet no one has come up with a cure for the common cold. These same scientists cannot effectively explain Earth's magnetic field (the force which causes one hand of a compass to point in a northern direction thereby establishing the directions of north, south, east and west) nor can these scientists explain the conditions which cause deserts to come about.

The Relativity of Time

Deserts are dry, barren, desolate regions which are consistently bypassed by rain. Yet, they believe and postulate as fact $E = MC^2$, and the relativity of Time and Space formulated in 1905 by Albert Einstein. Both formulas are based on the velocity of light, which is said to be 186,000 miles per second and is represented by the constant "C". Because it is believed that every object in the Universe is in motion, motion is said to be relative and based on one's frame of reference.

The relativity of time and space is represented by the formula (T)ime = the square root of $(1-V2/C2)$. This formula postulates that the closer an object's speed approaches the speed of light, the aging process lessens and the time traveling from place to place shortens. The classic example given to highlight this theory is the dilemma of the twins. According to this theory if one twin brother stayed on Earth while the other twin brother traveled in space at speeds up to 99 percent of the speed of light, after a period of seventy years, the brother who traveled in space would have aged ten years, while the brother who stayed on Earth would have aged by 70 years. Of course this projection is ridiculous. The relativities of time can only be based on a planet's or object's distance from the Sun and its orbit of the Sun. Since the Sun is the only known star to have orbiting objects, this subject must be confined to our Solar system. Our Solar system consists of the Sun and a host of orbiting celestial bodies including nine planets known as Mercury, Venus, Earth, Mars, Jupiter, Saturn, Uranus, Neptune, and Pluto. Each planet orbits the Sun at a different distance; each planet revolves on its axis at a different speed. And, each planet achieves its solar occurrences and its year at different paces. Therefore, the time that it takes the inner most planet

(Mercury) to revolve around the Sun, may take the outer most planet Pluto 1000 times more to accomplish the same task. Whatever time it takes a planet to orbit the Sun constitutes its year. It has been estimated that a year on Venus consists of only two days while a day on Mercury encompasses two years. Whether it takes 87.97 Earth days which is the calculated time of Mercury's year, or whether it takes 248 Earth years which is estimated time of Pluto's Year, the relativity of time can only be based on an object's orbit of the Sun, not on some absurd, theory on the projected speed of light.

One day on Mercury encompasses two years. Whether it takes 87.97 Earth days which is the estimated time of Pluto's Year. The relativity of time can only be based on an object orbit of the Sun. Not on some spaced out, groundless assertion concerning the projected speed of light.

In conclusion we of the African community must stop accepting what Western institutions are issuing as fact and we must start questioning and researching every aspect of the Ancient Egyptians and the Coptic Egyptian Moors knowledge base which has been corrupted and misaligned through European manipulation.

BOOK II
The Book of the Earth

Africa and Africans Misunderstood

BOOK II OUTLINE

Africa and Self Identification

Whenever you let others define who you are, your perception of yourself is based on the views of someone else. It does not matter whether that view is correct or perverted, you are no longer in control of your own identity. Africa and Africans have been the beating horse of the world for the last five centuries. Two Western religions claim to have brought civilization to Africa by imposing their values upon them. Africans nor any other society that was invaded by the Europeans was prepared for the lies, deception and duplicity that mentally put them in colonial bondage and tied their hands. This, subsequently, gave the Europeans unchallenged access to Africa's human and material resources. The previous mentioned tricks were completely foreign to the African mind.

Africa and Slavery

Whenever Africa is studied, sooner or later, one must come to terms with the African Slave Trade. In all of history, there has never been an institution more cruel, debilitating or deadlier than the African Slave Trade. The Europeans in justifying their injustice and atrocity toward the African race, accuse Africans of enslaving their own people. Africans never practiced slavery, nor did the native Americans, rather, these societies developed compensation systems which allowed individuals who were responsible for injury to others to pay off their debt to the victim, the victim's family or to the community in general. This approach to justice has proven to be much more sensible and efficient than locking the offender up because the offender becomes a help to the victim, rather than a liability to the community.

How is it that a whole race of people were deemed to be uncivilized savages? How is it that a whole continent was absurdly classified as being inferior? How is it that the name Africa has become synonymous with slavery, savagery and inferiority. Many of us subconsciously have bought into these contentions wholeheartedly. The title, descendent of slaves, is supposed to evoke the emotions of shame and embarrassment. Be resolved that there is nothing innately wrong about being a descendent of a slave. Slavery is not the result of genetics, therefore you are not born a biological slave. Slavery is not even a social or class designation.

Your previous position did not effect it and regardless of your efforts you could not transcend it. Slavery was and is a political state. Political in that a plan was devised and executed to diminish, oppress and subjugate people of African origin. After this was done, the appropriate institutions were evoked to maintain the oppression.

Many of us have a hard time understanding how the Europeans were able to trick various African communities into fighting one another and subsequently selling prisoners of each community. The European would provide each group with arms. They would also provoke each group with lies and create suspicion among them. Perhaps, the indigenous people of North America can provide us with valuable insight into the minds of the Europeans. The native American of North America has stated that the white man speaks with a fork tongue. The native American of South America called the white man by the name panikete, which means one who would kill his friends. As a result, if you are practicing a Western religion, you are subject to the same mental manipulation. If you are influenced or impressed by Western education, you are a victim of the same assimilation.

Africa and Western Religions

It is important for us to understand that the Western religious and educational institutions are designed to propagate Western philosophy. Christianity was supposedly brought to Africa to save the African from sin. But Christianity has never saved a person of African descent from anything. It has induced tens of millions of our people into a defenseless, mindless state of confusion. Christianity does not save. It enslaves. If Christianity saves anything, it saves what is deemed as Western civilization from being exposed as the great pretender. For as long as you are indoctrinated by the traps that are inherent within these belief systems, you will never question European philosophy. Western values will continue to be the standard by which you govern your life even to your own detriment.

The Nature of Western Education

The Western Educational Institutions compliment their Religious Institution in the assault on the African psyche. If there is one image of Africa that the Western World wants to portray, it is a continent completely void of any redeeming qualities. By equating intelligence to the development of a writing system, the European has convinced the world to dismiss Africa as a viable contributor to the world knowledge base. Ironically, the very tool that they claim Africa failed to create, is the same tool that the whole of Europe, and the rest of the world have failed to invent for themselves, an alphabet and a writing system. Thanks to Dr. Walter Williams, author of *The Historical Origin of Christianity* we can vividly see that the Europeans never produced a writing system of their own, but rather took as their own one of the Ancient Egyptian alphabets, taught to them by the Coptic Egyptians. We must understand that, unlike what Europeans would have us to believe, education is not universal, education is relative. Relative to the society in which you live. Regardless of that society's political or social organization, when you live in a native society that society will innately provide you with the tools and education that are essential to function properly within that society. Because people of African origin are not native to this society the Western educational system is more of a detriment than an aid especially when given its unique mission of destroying the true legacy of people of African origin. A B.S. in accounting is useless in herding cattle. A masters degree in U.S. history is worthless in planting and harvesting crops. A doctorate in philosophy is irrelevant if you have to survive off the land. When you adopt someone else's system and standards, you become the neophyte and low man on the totem pole. We must understand that the institutions of Western Education were brought to the so called third world cultures to provide these societies with just enough training to create a cheap labor force to help the Europeans deplete those countries of their natural resources.

On a higher and more deceptive level, when one studies in the Western Educational Institutions one is not educated but assimilated. The various degrees which a person obtains from these institutions has more to do with their degree of indoctrination than it has to do with their level of learning. As a matter of fact the higher the degree obtained the more the natural analytical abilities are arrested and substituted with perverted canned or programmed processes which are designed to protect and promote Western philosophy rather than solve problems.

Education is secondary. The Japanese unfortunately have totally accepted Western Education to the point that they demonstrate those prevailing racist tendencies that are innate in Western society. Yet despite this massive assimilation, the West will never be able to control the Japanese like they control so many nations and cultures of the world. The principal reason for this is that the traditional spiritual system of the Japanese remains intact. Unlike the cultures in Africa, South America and Central America, the Japanese for the most part have completely rejected Western religions.

There cannot be a more powerful relationship, than the association of man with his perception of his GOD or CREATOR. Consequently when the principle character or icon of your religion is racially different than you, but your oppressor and the people you respect as authorities are racially one in the same, you are in line to subjugate yourself. Because you are not one with your GOD racially, therefore you are different and inferior. Europeans are heads of everything deemed important and are portrayed as being identical with the image they propagate as God. This categorically creates a powerful association of white people as authority and white people as God.

Africans and The Lack of Clothing

Another reason why some people of African origin seem to be ashamed to be associated with Africa is because many African societies either wore a minimum amount of clothing or no clothing at all. Also it is to the advantage of Western society for their media to portray Africans on TV, or in movies with bones in their noses, or plates in their lips as if these expressions are the ultimate definition of a savage. We must stop viewing unfamiliar customs with Western eyes. Also we should not apply the corrupt deviated ideas and philosophies of the Western World to something that is very natural and pure. A bone in the nose is no different than having a bone or piece of gold in the ear lobe. In some African tribes this was and is an expression of fashion and beauty. Today it is fashionable for Europeans to pierce any part of their body including their breast, tongue and genitals. It is important to remember that the nature of this criticism is to get Africans to adopt Western standards so they can become more easily controlled.

It is also helpful to remember that the Monarchies of Europe on average took a bath only once a year. However, at this same time it was common practice for the members of many tribes in Africa to bathe daily.

A NAKED AFRICAN IN HIS ENVIRONMENT HAS TEN TIMES THE INTEGRITY AS A FULLY DRESSED EUROPEAN IN HIS ENVIRONMENT. Clothing, or the lack of, should never be the standard by which we judge a society. The original purpose of clothing was to protect oneself from the extreme elements whether those elements were excessively cold weather or excessively hot weather. If you live in an environment where the weather is conducive to a minimum amount of clothing, then so be it. In societies that required a minimum amount of clothing, the incident of rape and deviate sexual behavior was unheard of, as well as sexually transmitted diseases. Some of our African people have a problem with Africa because it did not go through an industrial revolution. We must understand that the Africans were completely satisfied with their condition. They put most of their energy in staying in tune with the Creator, and developing a creative and just social system. The fact that Africa did not go through an industrial revolution does not speak to a lack of intelligence, but it does speak of a respect for nature and a disgust for waste. The Industrial Revolution was started from home manufacturing to large-scale factory production, brought about by extensive mechanization of a production system. There was a price associated with the Industrial Revolution, and that price was not paid by the European. It was paid for by the African with four hundred years of force and free labor, four hundred years of forced relocation and four hundred years of the most brutal treatment in the history of man. Four hundred years of psychological torture, mass murder, and deception. You cannot have an Industrial Revolution without having an abundance of raw material and an abundance of cheap or free labor of which Africa and Africans initially supplied both. The Industrial Revolution was a system of slavery necessitated by greed. If it had not been for the advantage that free labor produced, there would not have been an Industrial Revolution. If it were not for the coming of the Ancient Egyptian Moors into Spain in 1051 A.C.E. with their knowledge of mathematics, science and medicine, there would not have been an Industrial Revolution.

Africans and Unique Social Systems

African societies in general incorporated social systems that featured shared responsibility. Have you ever wondered why people of African origin project such a strong feeling of family among each other. Many

African societies are driven by a phenomenon known as an Age Set System. This concept is probably one of the most dynamic and important social concepts ever devised. For it indoctrinates the initiated into a fraternal order that goes far beyond the boundary of a biological sibling in Western Society. Every year Rites of Passage are performed. These ritual are designed to allow the young adult to make the transition from adolescence to adulthood. In many ways this coming of age is symbolic of a renewal or new birth. With a substantial break from the past, the initiate leaves behind all those things that accompany them through their childhood. In many societies the hair is shaved off the head. The initiate also undergoes surgery without anesthesia. Circumcision is considered the most important part of the initiation process. Any young people whose ages fall within the qualifying range could petition their parents to allow them to be among the new initiates. After the initiation process begins, the initiate starts to receive the education that will transform them into adults. This training established a sense of family so strong that the initiate does not just become brothers or sisters in theory, but they become brothers and sisters in practice.

This new association does not last just for the duration of the initiation period, but rather for the rest of their lives. They transcended their various stages of life as one, from initiates to young adults, from young adults to elders. When any of their children said, mother or father, they would not necessarily be speaking of their biological mother or father. But anyone who was of the age of their parents or anyone who was considered an elder. Shared responsibility and shared obligation. No doubt these same tendencies were transferred to the United States during slavery. In the southern states this concept of extended family resurfaced. It was not rare for an adult not related to a child to chastise him if he was caught doing something wrong, without repercussions from the child's biological parents.

Africans and Medicine

Another concept or practice that is completely misunderstood and who's very mention conjures up feelings of embarrassment and resentment, is the African belief in witchcraft. Unlike societies in Europe individuals who were suspected of witchcraft in Africa were not confined exclusively to women, nor, were they beaten, tortured or killed. In reality a witch was only a perception. A witch could be anyone who was thought to have ill feelings for another person. If a person died, and he or she was neither very young or very old, witchcraft was thought to be the cause. If a person fell upon hard luck or misfortune, witchcraft was suspected. Whenever an African felt that he was the victim of a curse, an expert would be summoned to eradicate the curse. The modern term for this person would be exorcist. The African term is witchdoctor. Despite the impression the West would like to portray of these professionals, witchdoctors were not buffoons, clowns or fools. Rather they were highly trained specialists who were not only expert healers and herbalists, but psychologists as well. You see even then Africans were practicing what is now called wholistic medicine. They not only treated the body, but the mind as well. Therefore, if a person encountered mental problems or had an illusion of a physical problem, treatment would be prescribed whether it was a medical prescription, a placebo, or a sympathetic listener. We must be mindful of the fact that probably 90 to 95 percent of all medicines used today had their origin in the African rain forest. It was here where Africans devised similar treatment for many of the ailments that afflict us today. Only the medicines that are derived through genetic engineering can be deemed as having a separate origin. A rain forest contains a large variety and abundance of plants and animals. From this giant laboratory, certain species of plants and animals were analyzed and identified that could induce an abortion in unwanted pregnancies. They formulated remedies for all ailments including headaches to stomach aches, high fever to all other types of infections. Aphrodisiac were formulated and used to cure male sexual ailments such as erectile dysfunction and other issues.

Rightly, the belief in witchcraft in African societies can be viewed as a sociological principle which encompassed both a medical element as previously discussed and an insurance element. The insurance element ensured a person economical and social stability and it took the form of retribution. Retribution was made by the person who was accused of witchcraft, or it was made by the whole community. An accusation of witchcraft always incurred or accompanied some type of loss, whether it was the loss of a family member, the loss of some type of service, or a loss of property. All these factors, helped regulate the temperament of the community members, by discouraging competition and jealousy between neighbors. It fostered communal cooperation. Its main focus and desired results were in maintaining an even distribution of wealth within the community which in turn maintained social and political harmony. We Africans must come to terms with the fact that from a social perspective, barring the Ancient Egyptians, no other societies have come closer to a perfect society than the Africans. After all, the ultimate manifestation of how a people exist is viewed within its social realm.

Note: *What is called Modern medicine must be put into perspective.*

It probably would surprise most people to learn that organized modern Western medicine is a recent phenomena. It has a history of less than one hundred and sixty years. Before 1845 there were no medical schools and only sporadic independent developments in medicine. However, these achievements were merely rediscoveries of the lost medical knowledge of the Ancient Egyptian and the Coptic Ancient Egyptian Moors.

Just as the engineering feats of the Ancient Egyptians have not been matched by today's standards, nor have their medical achievements. The Ancient Egyptians had extensive knowledge of the human body. This knowledge included the function, size, location and shape of the body organs. In the preparation of the dead these organs were removed and examined as part of an embalming process that helped to connect cause with effect and symptoms with diagnosis. In addition, the Ancient Egyptians are said to have had sleep temples. These temples, were PROBABLY used to prepare the patients for surgery. The patients were put into a hypnotic trance and relaxed to a state where they would not feel the pain of the surgical knife. Their pulse was reduced to a level where there was no bleeding. Today some medical doctors are attempting similar procedures without success.

It is the intent of Western academia to make the world believe that the people who they deemed barbers actually practiced medical surgery. Even though Western academia claims that the first medical schools were developed in Europe in the 1100's, a period before the European Renaissance, there were no schools or educational institutions outside of the Catholic Church or any of its protestant derivative. Formal education was not formatted like it is today. Students were tutored from an early age to a predetermined level of proficiency. Formal education was private and it was reserved for the priest societies of the Roman Catholic Church, Greek Orthodox Church and the Anglican Church. In addition, royalty and nobility were admitted to these institutions. There were no grammar schools, no high school and no university.

However, before the European Renaissance it was illegal to dissect animals or human bodies for medical reasons. How could these people practice surgery when it wasn't until the 1600's that the English practitioner William Harvey is given credit for learning about the circulatory system? It was not until the 1500's that the Western practitioners learned certain things about the body including the location, size and shape of the body's organs. The medical fields which helped to define modern medicine were found as recently as the 19TH CENTURY. For example Immunology was founded in England in the1840's. Anesthesiology was also founded in the1840's in the United States. Pathology was found in Germany in the 1800's. Antiseptic was founded in Hungary in 1847. The American Medical Association was founded in 1847. What the barber profession can be given credit for, up to the turn of the century, is a practice known as bloodletting. Bloodletting was a deadly ineffective treatment used universally throughout Europe and the United States. This panacea involved cutting and bleeding an individual as the treatment for the patients ailments. Even now bloodletting is represented by the modern sign of the spiral red stripe on a white pole of the barber shop. This pole represents a bloody wound wrapped in white bandage.

Technology and science have their places but they are meaningless unless it can be applied in a social context. Technology alone can never denote civilization. Technology has very little to do with being civilized. A civilized society would never adapt the policy of survival of the fittest. Yet, this is the hidden policy of the Western world. That is a predator mentality. It is the mark of a savage and it is animalistic in character. In civilized societies nothing precedes the welfare of the people within the society. There is a high respect for life and the condition of the people within that society. To be civilized you must show compassion and humanity.

In Africa, true democracy was not just a theory, it was a reality. These were societies, that had a place for everyone. The very young, the able bodied, and the elderly. The elderly were always looked upon with respect.

These elders were charged with the responsibility of charting the course for the community and the duty of settling all disputes. Africans were the first conservationists. They practiced a market system that produced a minimum amount of waste. They took only what was needed. Whereas, the Western way, is to take as much as possible until the resources are depleted or the environment is damaged. Throughout all of Africa, there is an abiding respect for all things whether they are animated or not. In the spiritual world, it has been said that Africans worship their ancestors. The truth of the matter is that to the African there is more to life than just life, there was the after life.

Africans did not worship their ancestors, they respected them. Since each family member had a relationship with the deceased and the deceased by virtue of their transition are believed to have direct contact with the Creator, who better to serve as a medium to the Creator. If the living maintained the tradition of their forefathers, the ancestors were thought to speak favorably to the Creator on behalf of the living.

African Science/Steel Making in Ancient Sub-Saharan Africa

Carbon Steel is comprised or iron ore and a small percentage of carbon. A certain proportion of carbon between .02% and 2.1% can produce steel, which may be up to 1000 times harder than pure iron.

William Kelly of Eddyville, Kentucky is said to have invented modern steel-making back in 1847. Nine years later Englishman Henry Bessemer is said to have reinvented Kelly's method. However, a society in the area known today as Tanzania made high quality carbon steel more than 2000 years before Kelly's invention. The process that the Haya people invented included building a structure shaped like an upside down cone. This structure was made from the clay of termite mounds. Termite mound clay makes a great refractory material. These tribesmen filled the bed of the furnace with charred swamp reeds. They packed a mixture of charcoal and iron ore above the charred reeds.

The key to the Haya peoples process was operating the furnace at a very high temperature; this high temperature was achieved by having eight men seated around the base of the furnace, pumping air into this structure with hand bellow. "The air flowed through the fire in clay conduits. Then the heated air blasted into the charcoal fire itself. The result was a far hotter process than anything known in Europe before modern times." (22). There is an exhibition of the Haya people making carbon steel at The Field Museum in Chicago in the form of a large poster size photo.

African Art

Art for art's sake was never a part of African culture, therefore the concept of African art is a misnomer. Art in Africa cannot be identified without an associating function or subject. Art was never the subject itself, but rather the adjective or modifier of a subject. In most instances what is deemed African art was used to beautify, to dress up and to decorate practical utensils.

This expression was manifested through their architecture, and through the creation and design of their furniture, jewelry, tools, musical instruments and ceremonial masks. Various African communities approach their creative production differently while maintaining an underlying theme. Not all aspects of this creative production was designed to be aesthetically pleasing. African art is highly stylized, it is considered to be abstract, this is particularly the case when speaking about African Masks. African masks had a variety of uses, certain masks were used for healing, while other masks were used to ward off evil spirits. Masks were also used in dance and celebration.

Many African civilizations had secret societies. These societies consisted of craftsmen and specialists who were trained in a particular trade. The nature of those societies was to foster, promote and preserve the knowledge of their society and trade. Metal casting was one of those trades. Metal casting was performed in many regions in Africa. Gold and bronze seem to have been the metals of choice. Small metal figurines were used as weights. The lost wax method of casting was the technique used. The modern casting technique goes one step further than the lost wax method. In the lost wax method every casting is different, because the mold is destroyed in the making of the casting.

When one studies African culture, one will learn that African art was fully integrated with African culture. Many late nineteenth and early 20th century European artists were deified for emulating and mimicking what is known as African art. Artists such as Picasso and Monet........

Africa and the Development of Music

Music was so entrenched in African society that it complimented African culture as it facilitated African dance. Music as we know today has two developmental paths, but only one origin, Africa and Ancient Egypt. The Ancient Egyptians created the musical scale which is the foundation for all music. The driving and forceful rhythms of West Africa are the critical element of all popular music. The systematic structure of notational concert or symphonic music was the creation of Ancient Egyptians. The importance of music has remained, but it's function has changed under Western dominion. Music is tempo, pitch, harmony, and rhythm. The wind blowing through the branches of trees produces music. The waves pounding on the shores of an ocean beach is music. Music is the pulsation of sound. Rhythm is the driving force behind music. Without rhythm there would be no melody or movement, just silence or one long continuous tone.

Sound is created through friction, which produces vibration or sound waves. A medium is required to carry the source of the vibration to your ears and, most often that medium is air. Music or sound cannot exist in an environment void of air. In the Western world, music is a viable force behind the entertainment industry. It incorporates the recording and concert industries, TV, movies, and plays. It is used in the sale of products. It is also used at parties and at work. Music can be used to alter an individual's disposition from sadness and depression to happiness and euphoria. It is an extremely effective selling device. What makes African music in general and West African music in particular so influential are their rhythms. Just as the American Indians used smoke signals to convey a message visually, the African used the rhythm of a drum to communicate an idea through distances, before telecommunications.

Africans use of polyrhythm or complex polyrhythmic music can be defined as music that employs several distinctive motifs which are independent at one level, but are complimentary and integrated at another level. This phenomenon gives rise to syncopation which occurs when the weak part of the beat (upbeat) is accented rather than the strong part of the beat (downbeat). These elements give African based music that characteristic which is known as funk. When more than one rhythmic line simultaneously accents the weak part of the beat intentionally or unintentionally, that makes the weak part of the beat stronger than the downbeat that is natural syncopation or funk.

Multi-rhythm music helps facilitate dance that incorporates body movements that feature various regions of the body moving to separate rhythm lines. Head and neck gyrate to one rhythmic line. Arms, shoulders and hands move to a different rhythmic line. Midsection, torso, oscillating to yet another rhythm and legs and feet in time with still another rhythmic line. All of this makes for very elaborate dance.

Although Africans played a host of string and wind based instruments by far the predominate instrument they used was the drum. During slavery their musical talents were suppressed. Thereby reverting their musical expression back to a medium that could easily be simulated, the drum. Drums are easy to emulate. After the abolishment of physical slavery, the rhythms that were suppressed exploded on the scene of America and world music. This time it manifested itself in instruments never used before, such as trumpet, clarinet, saxophone, and trombone. Subsequently, giving birth to a series of new musical forms including Blues, Jazz, Spirituals, Soul, Rap, Reggae, and Latin rhythms which are all direct manifestations of African music.

Concert music is popularly believed to be the offspring of European culture. But after some true knowledge of our Ancient history, we can easily surmise that the historically nomadic, barbaric Europeans could not possibly possess the disposition, stability, nor the intellect to format and formulate a notational music system. But the Ancient Egyptians did.

The Ancient Egyptians created notational music like they created writing. They formulated a notational system which allowed them to develop and preserve music compositions and principles. After all they did create and invent the music scale. Even after the European completely adapted to concert and symphonic music, music from West Africa was called upon to breathe new life into concert music. The influence of West African rhythms on concert music culminated with the development of polyphony music in the sixteenth century in Europe. We must remember that Europe at this point had at the very least a two century relationship with Africa. That is enough time to forge the foundation for a new musical form. However, within the transitional period which oversaw the transfer of the world's formal knowledge base from the Coptic Egyptian Moors to the European as well as the total suppression of the Moors, the European also took over the development of formalized music.

Improvisation, which is a African trademark, gave old music rejuvenation and freshness because it altered an old composition with instant newness and creativeness. This concept in concert music is characterized by a technique known as a cadenza. In some cases it allowed a soloist free musical expression, imposing only time and harmony limitations.

In conclusion, living in the Western world, we are dominated by Western ideas and philosophies. We must always keep in mind that this society is not what it claims to be. By creating the subject known as history, the Europeans were able to categorize or define every culture throughout the world based on their own political agenda. Because of their barbaric past, they had to co-opt the legacy of the Ancient Egyptians as their own to convince the world that they were in line for the greatness they claim for themselves. The Western world uses four devices to control the world, massive deception, military force, religion and money. Since they cannot maintain a military presence wherever they have an interest, their religious and educational institutions commission native people as agents. These agents are trained to carry on the Western indoctrination. Western societies whole mode of operation concerning people of African descent is to keep our people reacting to allegations of inferiority, so that we end up occupying our free time disproving false charges, rather than probing, questioning and exposing the Europeans as their true past dictates to be a corrupt people with a stolen history.

BOOK III

THE BOOK OF THE SUN

ANCIENT EGYPT=THE SUN (RA), TIME, SPIRITUALITY AND CIVILIZATION

BOOK III OUTLINE

(A)

Moon Phases

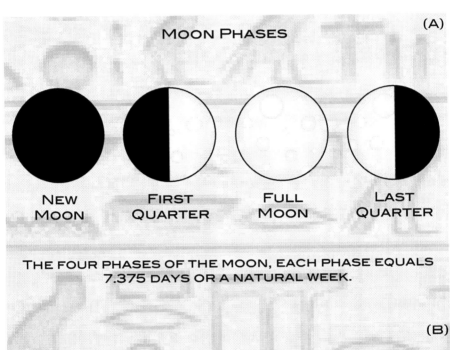

| New Moon | First Quarter | Full Moon | Last Quarter |

THE FOUR PHASES OF THE MOON, EACH PHASE EQUALS 7.375 DAYS OR A NATURAL WEEK.

(B)

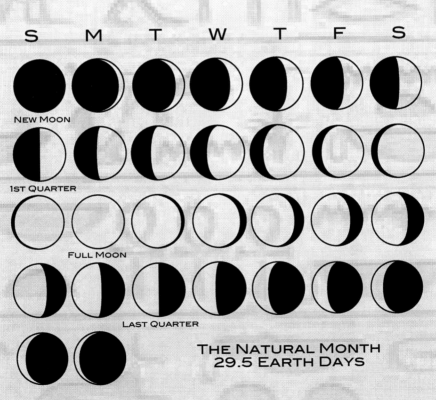

S   M   T   W   T   F   S

New Moon

1st Quarter

Full Moon

Last Quarter

THE NATURAL MONTH
29.5 EARTH DAYS

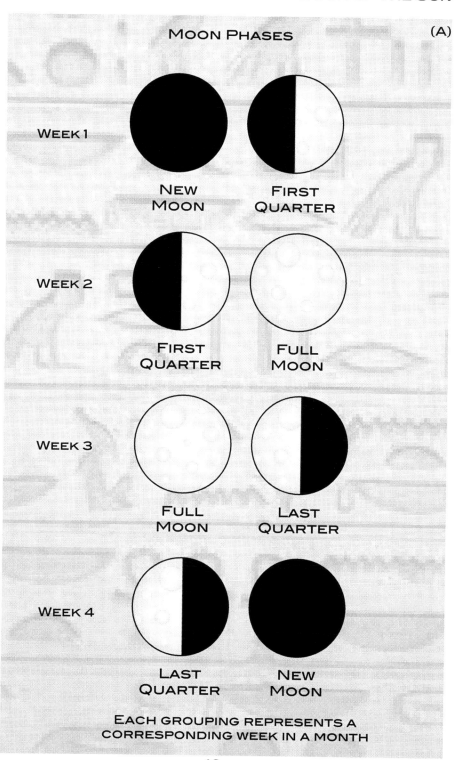

Moon Phases (A)

Each grouping represents a corresponding week in a month

(A)

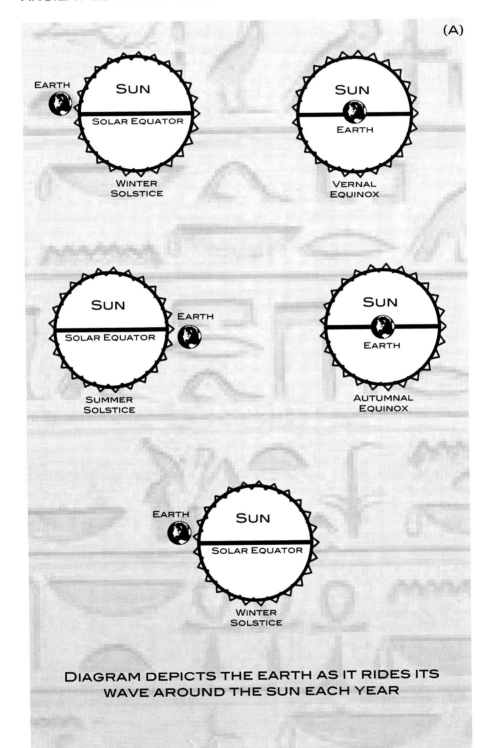

DIAGRAM DEPICTS THE EARTH AS IT RIDES ITS
WAVE AROUND THE SUN EACH YEAR

INTERACTION BETWEEN THE SUN EARTH AND THE MOON

(A)

IT TAKES THE MOON 29.5 EARTH DAYS TO REVOLVE AROUND THE EARTH. THIS PERIOD REPRESENTS ONE NATURAL MONTH.

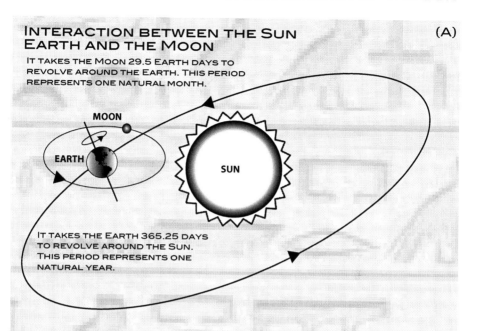

IT TAKES THE EARTH 365.25 DAYS TO REVOLVE AROUND THE SUN. THIS PERIOD REPRESENTS ONE NATURAL YEAR.

CHART OF SUNLIGHT DURATION OF THE FOUR SOLAR OCCURANCES

(B)

NORTHERN HEMISPHERE

SOLAR OCCURRENCE FIRST DAY OF:	WINTER SOLSTICE (WINTER)	VERNAL EQUINOX (SPRING)	SUMMER SOLSTICE (SUMMER)	AUTUMN EQUINOX (FALL)
DATES:	DEC. 21/22	MAR. 20/21	JUN. 21/22	SEPT. 22/23
SUNRISE:	7:16AM	5:56AM	4:16AM	5:40AM
SUNSET:	4:24PM	6:02PM	7:30PM	5:48PM
LENGTH OF DAY:	9HRS 8MINS	12HRS 6MINS	15HRS 14MINS	12HRS 8MINS
LENGTH OF NIGHT:	14HRS 52MINS	11HRS 54MINS	8HRS 46MINS	11HRS 52MINS

(A)

ARTIFICIAL MONTH CHART

GREGORIAN CALENDAR IS WIDELY USED THROUGHOUT THE WORLD, IT IS COMPRISED EXCLUSIVELY OF ARTIFICIAL MONTHS, WHICH MEANS THAT NONE OF THE MONTHS IN THIS SYSTEM ARE BASED ON THE 29.5 DAY LUNAR CYCLE.

A NATURAL MONTH IS BASED ON THE 29.5 DAY LUNAR CYCLE.

ARTIFICIAL MONTHS WITH 28 DAYS	ARTIFICIAL MONTHS WITH 30 DAYS	ARTIFICIAL MONTHS WITH 31 DAYS
29.5 DAYS * -1.5 DAYS**	29.5 DAYS * +.5 DAYS**	29.5 DAYS * +1.5 DAYS**
28 DAYS	30 DAYS	31 DAYS

FEBRUARY (MONTH)	APRIL (MONTH)	JANUARY (MONTH)
	JUNE (MONTH)	MARCH (MONTH)
	SEPTEMBER (MONTH)	MAY (MONTH)
	NOVEMBR (MONTH)	JULY (MONTH)
		AUGUST (MONTH)
		OCTOBER (MONTH)
		DECEMBER (MONTH)

(-1.5 X 1) = -1.5 +   (.5X4) =2 +   (1.5X7) =10.5 =11 DAYS

29.5 DAYS X 12 = 354 (LUNAR YEAR) + 11.25 DAYS = 365.25 (SOLAR YEAR)

(B)

ANCIENT EGYPTIAN NATURAL MONTH CHART

A NATURAL MONTH IS BASED ON THE 29.5 DAY LUNAR CYCLE.

NATURAL MONTHS

JANUARY (MONTH)
FEBRUARY (MONTH)
MARCH (MONTH)
APRIL (MONTH)
MAY (MONTH)
JUNE (MONTH)
JULY (MONTH)
AUGUST (MONTH)
SEPTEMBER (MONTH)
OCTOBER (MONTH)
NOVEMBER (MONTH)
DECEMBER (MONTH)

29.5 DAYS X 12 = 354 (LUNAR YEAR)
(LUNAR YEAR) + 1 11.25 DAYS (SOLAR YEAR)

Africa, Ancient Oriental Africa, the Ancient Nile Valley, Kemet, Ancient Ethiopia, Ancient Nubia and Ancient Egypt: These are many dimensions and names of the Creators of Civilization

Both modern and Ancient Egypt lie completely within the North Eastern region of the African continent. Today the ethnic makeup of Egypt is quite different from the ethnic makeup of its Ancient past. In a similar manner pre-Columbian America ethnically, looks quite differently from modern North America. The Ancient Egyptian society was monolithic while the Coptic and modern Egyptian society is pluralistic. Ivan Van Sertima described the current population of Egypt as being heavily influenced by latecomers and interlopers. Dr. Walter Williams stated the flood gate of Ancient Egypt was opened after the Greeks invaded Egypt, allowing hordes of groups to enter Ancient Egypt including the Parthian and Sassanid.

Modern Egypt's uniqueness is that it has had a pronounced and dramatic presence within its prominent Ancient past, primarily through the massive number of Ancient Architectural structures which still remain standing today. The structures at these sites are just as important and impactful today, as when they were built. Modern Egypt is said to be a part of the Middle East but it lies in the African continent. The Ancient Egyptians under duress of their Greek invaders, educated the Greeks directly through mentorship, and the Greeks learned indirectly by way of assimilation and absorption, subsequent European cultures inherit the Greeks elevated and later declining culture and knowledge base. As a consequence, Medieval and Renaissance Egypt through its Monophysite and Moorish moniker the Blackamoors reawakened Europe from the Dark Ages.

From the sands of the Sahara desert Coptic Egypt by way of the Greek Ptolemy's and Roman Emperors help give birth to the Western world's most powerful driving force, Western Religions. And, from Northeast Africa, Ancient Egypt created civilization and developed and gave birth to High Civilization.

Egypt, today, yesterday, and especially from its ancient past was and is an integrated part of both the African continent and African culture. Ancient Egypt was the benefactor of the critical human and fertile life blood which flowed from the interior of Africa, producing a cultural current that revolved between assimilation and accommodation,

47

alternating back and forth along the Nile basin. The political, social and cultural influences of Ancient Egypt extended along the coast of the Mediterranean Sea and beyond. (p.10)

Two of the most powerful and under utilized principles to describe and reference the Ancient Egyptians is the term Oriental and the Solar Principle. The University of Chicago early in its existence created and dedicated a museum (The Oriental Institute, on its campus) to Ancient Egypt and Mesopotamia. There is a definite trend by Western writers of ancient history to hinder or suppress any connections The Ancient Egyptians had with the Sun or the term Oriental. These terms would ultimately provide an unwanted pathway for the general public and the majority of Western scholars to discover and understand the true relationship between Ancient Egypt and the Sun and Ancient Egypt and Western Religions.

The answer to the question, Where and how did the Ancient Egyptians obtain their knowledge? The revelation to this question is not contained in the answer being offered by most of Western academia which implies that aliens from deep space, came to Earth to teach the Ancient Egyptians and build their civilization. This ridiculous and preposterous answer serves two purposes: 1- to deny the fact that the African of Ancient Egypt created a culture that civilized the world and 2- to hide the fact that they built their civilization by first creating a time concept and by studying nature and the interaction between the Earth and the Sun.

To orient or orientate, ultimately means to adjust or adapt to the Earths yearly journey around the Sun. The Ancient Egyptians or Oriental Africans were the original Orientals. They were the first to study the Sun and orientate themselves to the Sun, thereby allowing themselves to be governed by the environmental dictates of the Sun. The Ancient Egyptians established their governmental institutions based on their seasonal adaptation to the Sun.

Unlike the modern boundaries and border of Egypt today, the boundaries of Ancient Egypt were not confined to the artificial borders of the modern countries to its south, the Sudan and Ethiopia, nor limited to the modern border of Libya to its west. The Ancient Egyptian civilization extended nearly throughout the length of the Nile Valley encompassing both major branches of the White and the Blue Nile; the Nile River extends from the northernmost region of modern Egypt's delta region at the Mediterranean Sea, to the mountainous source of the Blue Nile in Ethiopia. The White Nile extends all the way through Egypt and the Sudan to the heart of Africa at Lake Victoria in Uganda East Africa.

A journey down the Nile today is like a journey back in time one hundred years and in more cases thousands of years. (p.136) Cruising the Nile River, between Ancient Cities, and on the Nile River Banks in rural areas, you will encounter, like in ancient times, living compounds comprised of mud brick homes, you may see men building and repairing these structures, children playing and bathing in the Nile, women drawing water from a perched bank of the Nile River and men fishing from dugout canoes. (p. 137,138) In the administrative districts, along the Nile, you will encounter Ancient port side cities comprised of massive Ancient temples and scores of large statues. This civilization in its totality is known as:

The Nile Valley Civilization and it consists of a variety of regions nestled in the Nile Valley whose people practiced and were a part of one culture. This culture created High Civilization and its history spans more than three thousand years.

Kemet is the name that the people who lived along the banks of the Nile River in Northeast Africa called themselves. It is said to be a direct translation from the Ancient Egyptians ideographic Pictorial Symbols which is said to mean Black Land or Land of the Blacks. In the first case, if the term Kemet means Black Land, this meaning would be referring to the banks of the Nile River after its annual inundation, leaving deposits of rich fertile black topsoil on the sandy desert banks. In the second case, if the term Kemet means Land of the Blacks, this meaning is referring to the physical characteristic of the people who live in this region, referring to the color of their dark skin and their racial identity.

Ancient Egypt and **Nubia** in many circles was/is considered to be comprised of the same culture and the same people. Nubia lies further into the interior of the African Continent. Today Nubia lies in the modern nation of the Sudan. The Ancient Egyptians themselves have stated their culture had its genesis from the South. And, if you were to look at the many monuments in Nubia, even though the Ancient Egyptians civilization and monuments are supposed to predate the Nubian culture by thousands of years, the monuments in Nubia seem to be prototypes for the Ancient Egyptians monuments. They seem to be of an earlier period, they are much smaller in dimension and they seem to be a more primitive version of their much larger counterparts in Egypt.

Finally, the names **Egypt** and **Ethiopia** are synonymous, and are now said to be derived from the Egyptian phrase htk,'PTH meaning the Soul of Ptah. This meaning refers to the home of the major Ancient Egyptian deity Ptah, at Memphis, Egypt. Memphis, Egypt is where the union of Upper and Lower Egypt occurred, creating the world's first nation and establishing Memphis as its capital. The head of this new nation whose title is now known as Pharaoh wore one crown that incorporated the insignias of both Upper and Lower Egypt, known as the Double Crown of Egypt. The term that the contemporary Greeks used for their Ancient Egyptian and/or Ethiopian counterparts was Aethiops, which means people with the Sun Burnt Faces. This descriptive title undoubtedly gave an account of the Ancient Egyptians physical presence as being quite different from the Greeks or their kind and clearly plants The Ancient Egyptians as an African people. But, what's even more important and pronounced, is that the Ancient Egyptians themselves left tens of thousands of dramatic images of themselves that leaves no doubt as to their African heritage. With the emergence of a new agenda, which began several hundred years ago, Western academia's shift in etymologies is part of a systematic movement to politically mask and undermine the African identity of the Ancient Egyptians.

Earth, Astronomical Rhythms, Oriental Africa and the Sun

The Ancient Egyptians were pragmatic; magic, mysticism, nor esoteric or abstract ideas was a corner stone of their culture. Logic, concrete natural principles with the practical application of the Solar principle, were their main and most powerful important motifs.

From Sunrise to Sunrise, to the New Moon through the Old Moon and from the December Solstice through the September Equinox and its accompanying season, the Oriental Africans who are better known as the Ancient Egyptians were concerned with new beginnings characterized as new birth. This new birth always manifested itself as a component of the natural year, Earth's orbit of the Sun. The Sun was the focal point throughout Ancient Egypt; new birth was represented as fundamental rhythms which were indicators of forthcoming natural cycles. These cycles were subsets of the natural year and divided the year into more manageable and easier recognizable time periods. Their purpose was and is to gauge the Earth's advancement into its orbit of the Sun or the year (time periods associated with astronomical occurrences and geological events), resulting in the concepts of the year: seasons, months, weeks, and days.

Universal academic doctrine dictates that the Oriental Africans based their time concepts on astrological principles. Contrary to this exoteric view, this is far from the truth. The Ancient Egyptians did not base their time concepts on, what astrology has been convoluted into today, theosophical principles; nor were their time principles based on contrived arbitrary historical events or personalities. Today the Ancient Egyptians time system is esoteric and hidden primarily because The Ancient Egyptian time system is actually based on reoccurring astronomical cycles. The Ancient Egyptians, who I deem today as the first and original naturalists, discovered and institutionalized the principles inherent within these cycles as the critical elements in the development of the world's first civilization. These natural rhythms include the natural year, the orbital period of Earth around the Sun, the natural month, the orbital period of the Moon around Earth, and the natural day, Earth revolving once on its axis. The four GEO/SOLAR OCCURRENCES and the four lunar phases are divisions of the natural year and month respectively which are cyclical as well. (p.43, p.44) The study of natural rhythms served as the foundation for the Ancient Egyptians calendar system; the calendar system was symbolically encoded as the Ancient Egyptians spiritual system (their creation story).

Evolving, as a result of these systems were the Ancient Egyptians three writing systems. Together these systems established the foundation for their high civilization and the Ancient Oriental Egyptian as the creator of civilization.

As we enter a new decade, a new century and the new millennium it must be highlighted, emphasized and reaffirmed that nature is the source of true knowledge. Knowledge, derived from nature, can manifest itself in two forms; innately, through ones ancestral memory, or directly, through ones conscience learning via the study of the environment. Since ones ancestral memory is subjective and may vary depending on the individual, it may be impossible for ones' findings or conclusions to be consistently verified by outside observers. Therefore, emphasis must be given to the study of the Earth and its environment, subjects where everyone can find a common ground. Findings from these objective and consistent subjects can easily be observed, verified, and measured by careful observation. The scientific study of the universe is the standard by which one can obtain true knowledge.

Nature, not perverted Western institutions, is the ultimate teacher; and Nature, not perverted Western educational institutions, is the ultimate source of knowledge.

Once these powerful and immutable facts are universally understood by Africans, African descendent scholars, and the rest of the non-Western world. Then as descendants of the pioneers of this knowledge, people of African descent must take responsibility and possession of this heritage by circumventing perverted Western sources and returning to the true origin of knowledge.

Man's quest for knowledge is indelibly linked with the study of the Earth and nature.

Western institutions, in their most basic form, are perverted vestiges of their Ancient Egyptian origins. Ancient Egyptian institutions, in their purest forms, symbolically represented natural, geophysical and cosmic occurrences.

In their attempt to enlighten the world, and through their keen observations of nature, the Ancient Egyptians were able to amass and catalogue information that was used to adjust and adapt to their environment. However, Western institutions, including educational institutions, have deceived the world through indoctrination and outright lies into believing that nothing of value can be learned outside of their hallowed doors.

The irony of this notion is that:

Western institutions most crucial role is to mask the African origins of the Ancient Egyptians, while it perverts historical information pertaining to the African origin of Civilization.

The hidden principles behind Western religions originates from Ancient Egypt. The source of Western institutions' true foundational knowledge base is Ancient Egypt. And, the aggregation of the most fundamental and powerful concepts in natural science, including the formulation and development of formal political and social organizations, are readily available to anyone who, like the ancient Egyptians the ultimate naturalists, is willing to observe nature in general and specifically the interactions between the Sun, Earth and the Moon.

Note: *All references to the Winter Solstice pertain to the December*

Solstice. The Ancient Egyptians based their New Year on the December Solstice. The period from the December Solstice to the December Solstice encompasses 365 days 6 hours 13 minutes and 53 seconds. A natural year. A Natural month's elapsed time is 29 days 12 hours 44 minutes and 2.7 seconds. A natural week consists of one quarter of a natural month, its endurance being 7 days 9 hours 10 minutes and 56.64 seconds (7.3826 days).

The Architecture and Monuments of Ancient Egypt

A realm which epitomizes Ancient Egypt is its architecture. The Ancient Egyptians were the most prolific builders of the Ancient World. For thousands of years their massive structures have endured the elements. They built three principle classes of structures: pyramids, temples, and subterranean burial chambers. In many instances these various structures were an integral part of the communities that constituted Ancient Egypt.

Note: *Western academics have made many attempts to make the Ancient Egyptians appear to be ruthless, by claiming that newer administrations in ancient times tried to take credit for temples and monuments that were already in place. The Ancient Egyptian Temples and Pyramids were not built at just any location; they were only built on sacred or holy grounds. Locations that had some kind of astronomical significance. That is why most of these sites incorporated many complexes relating to and representing different ancient administrations, in some cases generations apart.*

In the United States The Washington Monument, The Viet Nam War memorial, the Korean War memorial, the World War II War memorial and the Martin Luther King memorial are all monuments that were added to the National Mall within a forty year period in the same manner that the Pharaohs added monuments to or maintained monuments at the sacred sites in Egypt. Yet no one is accusing the latest national administration in the United States of stealing credit from older administrations. (Of course these types of statements are diversions and calculated distractions).

Pyramids are the first and most important of the three major classes of structures built in Egypt during ancient times. Although pyramids and temples are found throughout the world, their origin is exclusively from,

Ancient Egypt. They are the most recognized structures of ancient times, overshadowing the so called Roman/Greece Architecture exponentially in scale, volume, quantity and structural sophistication. There are more than forty-five major pyramids in Egypt. Cairo is the site of the four most famous structures on Earth; the Great pyramid of Giza, the Second pyramid of Giza, the Third pyramid of Giza, and of course the Great Sphinx of Giza. The Great Pyramid (The pyramid of the Sun), the largest pyramid on Earth, along with the entire Giza Complex are the greatest engineering achievements in the history of humankind. At its base the Great pyramid has a width of 754.40 ft. and a length of 754. ft., it obtains a height of 478.88 ft. and its angle is 51 degrees, 50 minutes 35 seconds.

There are estimations which claim that the Great Pyramid (The Pyramid of the Sun) was constructed from two million three hundred thousand to three million interlocking stones, precisely cut, and strategically placed, averaging 2.5 tons each. The Great Pyramid of Giza sits on 13.0651 acres, occupying 569,119 square feet and displacing 90,755,779 cubic feet of ground and air space. (p.125B, p.134B)

At its apex the Second pyramid of Giza (The Pyramid of the Earth) exhibits a cap of polished stone that once provided a casing that covered each of the Giza complex pyramids; at its base the Second pyramid of Giza is 703.54 ft. squared. It reaches a height of 470.68 ft. and its angle is 53 degrees 7 minutes 48 seconds. Because its angle is sharper than the Great Pyramid, it appears to be taller. Although the dimensions of the Second pyramid of Giza are close to the Great Pyramid in height and at its base, its exterior stones are much smaller. It sits on 11.3629 acres of land, occupying 494,968 square feet and displacing 77,579,605 cubic feet of ground and air space. (p.124B)

Although the Third pyramid of Giza (The Pyramid of the Moon) is significantly smaller than the Great and Second pyramids of Giza (The Pyramid of the Sun and Pyramid of the Earth) it still remains as one of the truly remarkable structures of ancient times; the Third pyramid of Giza is 344.40 ft. squared at its base, it obtains a height of 214.84 ft. and its angle is 51 degrees 20'25". The Third pyramid of Giza resides on 2.7229 acres, occupying 118,611 square feet and displacing 8,485,660 cubic feet of space. (p.124A, p.134A)

The pyramid field of Dashur is another important pyramid site, which contains four major pyramids called "Bent," "Blunted," "False" and the "Red" Pyramids. The dimension of the base of the Red Pyramid 721.60

feet sq. is surpassed only by the Great Pyramid of Giza. Its angle is 43 degrees 22 minutes and its height is 341.12 feet. The Red Pyramid resides on 11.9537 acres, occupying 520,706 square feet and has a volume of 59,148,599 cubic feet of space.

Saqqara is the site of the step pyramid; this pyramid is thought to be the first major stone structure ever built. The step pyramid does not have a square base like the pyramids of Giza, its base is rectangular. Two sides of this pyramid are 459.20 ft. long while the other two sides are 387.04 feet long, it also has a height of 196.80 ft. This pyramid resides on 4.08 acres, filling 177,728 square feet and displacing 11,647,348 cubic feet of space. (p.126-127)

Note: *One of the most interesting Ancient Egyptian structures is the Obelisk. Obelisks are tall slender structures that normally enhance and compliment other structures (such as the Ancient Egyptians Temples). The unfinished obelisk of Aswan best illustrates the presence of these objects, it is currently lying in its cradle where it was being engineered from a huge slab of bed rock thousands of years ago. This site gives the world direct knowledge of how these tremendous monuments were built. The unfinished obelisk of Aswan is by far the largest, tallest and heaviest obelisk ever made from a single block of stone, it would have been approximately 137 feet tall and weighed approximately 1200 tons...*

Note: *The Ancient Egyptians Obelisks and the Pyramids of Ancient Nubia share an interesting characteristic, they are both very steep in their angular profile.*

Obelisks are tall monolithic structures that are cut or carved from a single block of stone; a pyramid culminates at the top of these structures. The height of an Obelisk is multi-times their base width. The Pyramids found at ancient sites inside Egypt are massive structures that are the composite of Tens of thousands of stone and in some cases millions of stones. Their height is in proportion to the width of their base, which is a fraction of their base length. The pyramids of Nubia seem to be a composite of the Pyramids and Obelisks of the Ancient Egyptians. Like the pyramids of Ancient Egypt they are comprised of tens of thousands of cut stones, but also like the Ancient Egyptians Obelisks the height of the Nubian Pyramids is multi-time their base width.

Today The Ancient Egyptians Obelisks can be found in New York City, London, Paris, Istanbul, Israel and Poland. A gigantic replica of an Ancient Egyptian Obelisk can be found in Washington D.C., The Washington Monument. And a gigantic stylized version of an Ancient Egyptians Obelisk sits in Paris France, the Eiffel Tower. Eight out of the Eleven Ancient Egyptian Obelisks found in Italy are in Rome and at the heart of Catholicism in Vatican City, Saint Peter's Square, an Ancient Egyptians Obelisk sits at its center. Esoterically, it seems that most major seats of European power and many international cities worldwide symbolically get their legitimacy from the Ancient Egyptians by having an Ancient Egyptian monument replica in its presence.

Many European scholars have designated The Ancient Egyptians Pyramids as burial chambers for past pharaohs. Another faction of scholars believe these pyramids were primarily used for astronomical observation. I strongly agree with both positions. Since these structures are found on the west side of the Nile, there is a definite strong funeral component and, additionally, I would emphasize the use of these pyramids as giant gauges working as solar markers and stellar observatories. The Great Sphinx of Giza completes the Giza complex; it is the largest statue of Antiquity. The Great Sphinx has the Head of a human and the body of a lion. It is 66 feet high, its shoulder span is 38 feet and it is 240 feet long. (p.125A)

Note: *Despite its massive size the Great Sphinx at Giza receives more attention because it is missing its nose. However, this phenomenon of the missing nose is not unique to the Great Sphinx. When I visited Egypt in 1992 about 30% of all the Pharaonic, or male statues, if not more, within the Cairo Museum of Antiquity were missing their noses. By removing their large and prominent noses, an African characteristic, this action would help hide their racial identity. We must remember that the explanation given by Western academia is politically motivated to hide the real reason behind these desecrations. It is obvious that Great Sphinx and other monuments were disfigured to hide the fact that the Ancient Egyptians and their descendants were and still are an African people.*

Note: *The step pyramids of Meso America along with the gigantic royal African head stone found in Mexico and those throughout Central*

America provide undisputed proof of the Ancient Egyptian presence and influence in the Americas. The pyramids in Mexico are second only to the pyramids in Egypt; however, these pyramids are not true pyramids; their foundations consist of mounds of rubble and dirt. The pyramid of the Sun at Teotihuacan near Mexico City is 738 feet squared and has a height of 213 feet, resides on 12.5 acres, occupying 544,644 square feet and has a volume of 38,669,172 cubic feet. The pyramid of the Moon has slightly smaller dimensions. Both pyramids reside in the massive pyramid complex at Teotihuacan, known as the Avenue of the Dead. Both pyramids are modular, futuristic looking structures. A series of smaller flattop step pyramids forms the Avenue of The Dead which leads from the Pyramid of the Sun to the Pyramid of the Moon. The Pyramid of the Moon is accompanied by eleven smaller pyramids together totaling the all-important number twelve. The Pyramid of the Sun sits at the opposite end of this avenue as the equalizer or Sum of the twelve pyramids of the Moon.

The pyramid at Cholula is given the claim as the largest pyramid on Earth which is 1150 sq. feet and has a height of 210 feet. This pyramid resides on 30.3604 acres comprising 1,322,500 square feet. The formula used to calculate the volume of a pyramid is ($V=1/3$ bh). This formula yields the Cholula pyramid a volume of 92,482,425 cubic feet which is about 1,726,646 cubic feet greater than the volume of the Great Pyramid. However, because the Cholula pyramid is a step pyramid and is not symmetrical in form the formula $V=1/3bh$ overstates the true volume of the Cholula pyramid enough for the Great Pyramid of Egypt to challenge its claim as the largest pyramid on Earth.

The second major class of structures found at Ancient sites in Egypt are Temples. Temples are the only structures that were designed to house the living. Remains of these temples are spread throughout the Nile Valley. Temples were the seat of the Egyptian government, they were also the homes of the council of priests and priestess who were the regional administrators, but what's most important is that these temples were and are the main home of the Ancient Egyptians permanent knowledge base. The temple main of (AMON-RA) at Karnak is the most imposing structure of its type. The entrance of the temple of Ra(The Sun) is highlighted with two long rows of facing sphinxes, this path is known as the Avenue of the Sphinx. The Avenue of Sphinxes serves as a powerful prelude to the main pylon at the Karnak complex. The temple of Ra is comprised of four huge pylons, a Great Court, The Great Hypostyle Hall, and a central court, while it is missing its ceiling and many walls, this does not take away from its grandeur. The Karnak complex encompasses a vast conglomeration of secondary temples, a series of tall obelisks, huge statues plus a beautiful reflecting pool. Within the main temple stands a forest of towering columns, reminiscent of the giant Redwood trees of California, these columns once supported the main temple stone roof. The Great Hypostyle Hall occupies an area of 6,400 square yards. A total of 134 huge columns resides in this hall, twelve pairs of super columns divides the hall into two sections creating the Grand Colonnade. Each of the twelve columns sits on a 3½ foot high pedestal and is 69 feet tall and has a diameter of four feet. The Karnak complex is a multi-generational effort that covers an area of .8 by 1.5 kilometers. (p.131B-132A)

The temple of Luxor is another major temple, it is near the temple of AMON-RA. Luxor contains a series of large statues and obelisks. Luxor is now the site of Chicago house, a research component of the University of Chicago. The proposed mission of this research team is to interpret , catalogue and archive all of the known glyphs of Ancient Egypt.

Note: *If one studied pictures taken in Egypt shortly after the invention of the camera and compared those pictures with pictures currently coming out of Egypt, it would be immediately apparent that those who claim to be cataloguing the glyphs of the Ancient Egyptians and reconstructing the great monuments of Ancient Egypt are actually altering some of these writings and structures, in order to support Western philosophy and white supremacy by removing Ancient Egypt African identity.*

On the West Bank of the Nile where once stood a temple, two gigantic seated statues, known as the Memnon Colossal remain. At 63 feet high, these colossal rival the monuments of Abu Simbel . While the faces of the Colossals have deteriorated, at least one seems to have been the face of a Falcon (Horus.) (p.129A)

The Ramesseum, the ruins of the huge temple in the valley of the kings, attributed to "Rameses II", is the site of four standing column figures of Osiris (Ausara). On the ground beside these huge monuments lie the remains of the once free standing colossal statue of "Rameses II".

This magnificent statue was said to have been carved from a block of granite believed to have weighed 1,000 tons. The statue measures around 60 feet in height (75 feet, including the crown) and it has a shoulder span of 22 feet.

The Temple of Horus in Edfu is the second largest temple in Egypt, and the most complete example of an Ancient Egyptian temple in existence. From this temple, exudes a feeling of power; perched outside of the facade of this temple are two huge statues of Horus, the symbolic falcon deity of the Ancient Egyptians. One crowned Horus Bird is posted in the courtyard, while another lies on its stomach before the entrance of the temple. This temple is an excellent source of rare hieroglyphic symbols.

Note: *The temple of Horus is among a host of other Ancient Egyptian temples deemed to have been built by the Greek Ptolemies, better said that these structures were constructed during the Ptolemaic period , by the architects and engineers of the Ancient Egyptian priest society. It was not until the European Renaissance and after the expulsion of the Coptic Egyptian Moors from Europe that the Europeans became proficient enough in their adaptive knowledge base to sustain themselves intellectually and academically in this area.* (p.129B, p.130, p.131A)

On the West Bank of the Nile, sits a very modern looking temple that seems to be etched in the mountain; this structure is known as the mortuary temple of Queen Hatshepsut. This temple is unique because it is a tri-level structure, while the majority of the temples built in ancient Egypt were single level structures. (p.128)

The two Massive temples at Abu Simbel are carved in the mountain, they are unique because the Temple, identified as Ramses II is designed as four seated gigantic statues of Pharaoh Ramses II. These colossal are 65.60 feet high, and together are 82 feet wide. The temple that is known as Queen Nefertari, is designed with six walking figures standing about 32 feet in height. Between 1964 and 1968, both temples were dismantled and moved 65 meters higher, and 210 meters further away from the Nile River, because they were threatened by the higher water of the new high dam at Aswan. (p.132B, p.133) Other important Temple sites in upper Ancient Egypt include Philae, Kom Ombo and Esna.

Note: *Although a great amount of effort was used to save Abu Simbel,* *the high dam at Aswan may serve more of a political function than a historical one. Today many temples and other monuments are dissolving in and under water as a result of the flood waters of the high dam. These structures are further into the interior of Africa and the statues of this region have what is deemed even more pronounced African features than statues in other Ancient sites within Egypt. These monuments probably could be used to unlock more of the mysteries of Ancient Egypt.*

Subterranean burial chambers are the third class of structure that Ancient Egyptians built. Subterranean burial chambers are believed to be the burial chambers of choice for Pharaohs of later periods. The Nile river was the demarcation line which divided the Nile valley into two regions. The valley of the living on the east bank and the valley of the dead on the West Bank. The East Bank of the Nile river represents the temples dedicated to the living because the Sun rises in the East and the West Bank of the Nile river represents the temples dedicated to the dead because the Sun sets in the West.

The Valley of the Kings exist on the West Bank of the Nile, it is the home of funeral temples and the resting place for deceased pharaohs. The subterranean cabins contain the remains of the various pharaohs, along with some of their personal belongings. These chambers also contain art works which depict many important concepts in the Ancient Egyptian culture. The most important and famous example of this type of burial chamber is that of Tutankhamun whose burial chamber was found complete and uninterrupted in 1922; the body of the pharaoh was found encased in layer after layer of masks and body shape coffins. Many of these coffins are layered with gold foil and the facial mask made of solid gold. The tomb included many of the things that Tutankhamun used in his daily life, and the many things that he would need in his afterlife. Most, if not all of the other known pharaonic burial chambers have been looted of their precious metals and stones. (p.122-p.123)

Beyond the previously mentioned practices of modern cultures around the world, creating and pairing their local monuments with the architecture of the Ancient Egyptians there is an additional dimension that pairs monuments built in the United States to the monuments of Ancient Egypt. The seated Jefferson and Lincoln monuments located at the National Mall parallel the Memnon colossal found in the Valley of the Kings. The Mount Rushmore monuments, located in South Dakota, are the four colossal structures of president Washington, Jefferson, Lincoln and Theodore Roosevelt. These US presidents carved in the mountain, parallel the four seated pharaonic structures carved into the face of the mountain at Abu Simbel.

Note: *Once again this type of emulation speaks of paying tribute to the creative source of the culture that created civilization.*

The Ancient Egyptian Temples, Sacred carvings, primitive scripts, scrolls, books and libraries

The word hieroglyphic in Greek means sacred carvings. The Greeks consider the Ancient Egyptians hieroglyphic script as sacred and holy writings, and indeed they are, for all of high civilization is based on this original script. The Ancient Egyptian hieroglyphic script is an offshoot and subset of their spiritual system, its tenets manifested through graphic symbols. These symbols are pictorial in nature, and in most cases are not to be taken literally for they are mnemonic or memory aids. These mnemonics are simple and familiar symbols which singularly or in varying combinations may represent a one to one idea transfer. In other instances, they may represent a one to several exchanges of ideas. Today the phonetic alphabet is the alphabet used by Western society. Before the Ancient Egyptians created the phonetic alphabet, they created or used more tangible forms of writing. These writings include scripts done with drawings, pictures, paintings and finally, ideographic pictorial symbols known as the hieroglyphic script. Initially, the ideographic pictorial symbols may have expressed a literal portrayal of events that actually transpired. However, after time progressed and civilization advanced, the meaning behind these symbols automatically became abridged because in most instances their meaning expanded beyond their original iteration. The contents of these symbols at this point seem to contract and become figurative and more of a summary and a memory aid.

As a point of reference the definition of any given set of words found in the modern dictionary can change or expand after a period of time. Likewise, during the course of more than three thousand years of uninterrupted history and as a course of social development the meaning of any given set of the Ancient Egyptians script could have changed or expanded.

The pictorial alphabet and writing system served as the prelude to a higher civilization. Without an pictorial alphabet one cannot have a non-graphic writing system; without a writing system, one cannot have a significant accumulation of knowledge which goes beyond a few generations. Also, without an alphabet, there cannot be an accumulation or a building block progression of documented knowledge. The generalities, observations, conclusions, summaries and, detailed discoveries of the previous generations cannot be preserved beyond a few generations. Therefore, knowledge cannot build to a level conclusive to further expansion by future generations. Without an alphabet or writing system, accumulated knowledge cannot be used to generate and formulate the principles, theories and axioms necessary to promote disciplined growth and development. Subsequently, each generation is destined to rediscover many of the same principles rather than advance some of these principles to a higher level.

The importance of the Ancient Egyptians temples to civilization is unmistakable, especially as they relate to the deployment of the hieroglyphic script. What's amazing about these structures, besides their massive size and their ingenious architecture, is that they are inundated with graphics and are adorned with writings so as to resemble what is known to us as books or encyclopedias, only etched in stone. The outer walls, the inner walls, ceilings, as well as the huge columns, which seem to have been designed not only to support the ceiling but to add a significant amount of additional writing space, every inch of these temples is crammed with information. These monuments were temples of knowledge and with their capacity for volume are the gigantic forerunner and progenitors of books.

One of the greatest feats of Western academia is to lure the uninitiated into a mental state that suggests the way things operate in modern Western society is the way things were done in Ancient times. This illusion in most instances is far from the truth, which explains why so many historical claims which are fallacies were accepted without being seriously vetted and challenged.

One of these fallacies includes the groundless stories claiming that the Greek philosophers namely Plato, Socrates and Aristotle wrote thousands of books before and during the time of the Greek Ptolemies. Dr. Walter Williams the innovative ancient history researcher has proclaimed that the Greek philosophers are incarnated characters and predated implants. The nature of the incarnated three principle Greek philosophers is to establish the Greeks as the creators of civilization by suggesting, with the incarnated books, they created math and the sciences as well as developed history and philosophy. Books were not created until the fourteenth century A.D. after the invention of the printing press. Furthermore, like hundreds of other incarnated names these characters were predated and planted into history to control world and Ancient History. An additional fallacy which revolves around the groundless stories claiming that a great library of Egypt was created and later destroyed, a building supposedly containing hundreds of thousands of scrolls representing the works of Greek philosophers and historians as well as the accumulated works of other cultures around the world and of course what's most important is that this building was supposed to contain, the collective secret knowledge of ANCIENT Egypt.

The Great Library of Egypt never existed because the Ancient Egyptians did not use scrolls to keep their permanent and important knowledge

A library is defined as a room or building housing a collection of books usually arranged in some kind of order. It would be next to impossible to create a practical or functional library based on scrolls. Are we to believe that each scroll (sheet) constituted a book of today? A small cylinder of paper, with no practical place to put a book title, subject matter or an author's name on the outer side of the document, there was also no place to put any type of index symbol to catalog and store these documents. In other words, there would be no way to easily retrieve or categorize specific sections of information, just piles and piles of disorganized, unformatted documents that must be unrolled to access their very limited content.

There were no books at this time, because there was no need for books. Books were meant to be published and distributed to a mass literate population. From the time of the inception of the Ancient Egyptians civilization to the time of Renaissance Europe, the only people in these societies who were literate to any degree, were the people who were part of the Ancient Egyptian Temple System and later the people who were part of the European monarch and Universal Church.

Thus, this whole notion of a Great Library of Egypt was invented to support the nonexistent Greek philosophers, namely Plato, Aristotle and Socrates. Collectively these Greek philosophers supposedly wrote thousands of books that were supposedly housed in the fictitious great library. Moreover, if these Greek philosophers existed and their books existed, then, where are their books today?

Where are the original versions of these books?

Who transcribed and how were these books adapted from the original version?

How were these books published?

How many books were published under each title?

The problem is that these documents in whatever form never existed. That is one of the reasons why this fictitious Great Library was invented to house these fictitious books, and also this is why it is said that this fictitious Great Library was totally destroyed by fire, to avoid producing those books and to answer the question, what happened to these books? Another reason why the Great Library of Egypt was said to have existed and was then destroyed was to add veils of mysticism over the Ancient Egyptian legacy. If these books never exist, then the Greek philosophers who supposedly wrote those books never existed. If the Greek philosophers never exist, then the whole of "Western Civilization" is a force without an origin of its own.

The Ancient Egyptians' permanent knowledge base was written on stone, on the walls, ceilings, floors and columns of the Ancient Egyptian temples throughout Egypt. The Ancient Egyptians Temples along with other structures such as pyramids, obelisks, giant statues and subterranean burial chambers were and are the home of the Ancient Egyptians' permanent knowledge. As evidence of this assertion, one only has to visit Egypt and witness the overwhelming proof that is documented and displayed in and on these monuments. At the same time, it will become obvious that scrolls comparatives are fragile and delicate and will disintegrate after being exposed to air after a significant period of time. It is for this reason that after thousands of years, original papyrus scrolls are rare and extremely hard to find. The use of papyrus or scroll was for temporary and immediate use which was in many cases consumed and disposed of in the executions of daily activities, and in other instances, because papyrus scrolls are lightweight and portable, they were used in the deployment and the transportation of the Ancient Egyptians knowledge base as they traveled around the world.

Subsequently, the secret and permanent knowledge of the Ancient Egyptians is not lost nor was it destroyed as commonly believed, but is boldly on display today locked in and on the major structures of the Ancient Egyptians. And, if much of this knowledge remains secret, which is the case, it is partially because of the missing temples or other structures that are underwater, destroyed, or yet to be discovered, in addition to the hieroglyphic script, which has only barely been deciphered.

The fact that the Ancient Egyptians wrote on scrolls is evidence that this temporary medium was used for daily communication and correspondence, much as we use newspapers, note pads, letters and e-mail today. It is evident, writings (Hieroglyphic script) etched in stone was institutionalized as the Ancient Egyptians permanent knowledge base.

Western academia has created such a powerful paradigm that even after most people become awe-struck by these Ancient Temples of Egypt and after they become eye witnesses to these great structures, they should not question, where and what medium the Ancient Egyptians used to store their permanent knowledge. It should be obvious, they carved it in stone. These great structures have become inconsequential in the eyes of the world. Simply because Western academia staged incarnated characters in Ancient History, to state that a Great Library of Egypt was created to store papyrus scroll as their books, and as their permanent knowledge base, what turns out to be temporary documents written on a disposable medium. For the whole world to be deceived away from what is concrete, practical, obvious, and logical is duplicitous. By giving papyrus and the fictitious burning down of the Great Library of Egypt false credit and recognition for the Ancient Egyptians knowledge base is criminal.

Finally, the Ancient Egyptians temples of knowledge illustrates a complete integration of subjectivity with objectivity, the practical with the aesthetic, and technology with the environment. They incorporate art with writing, writing with architecture, creating temples of words carved in and made from stone. It is quite apparent that these temples were the center of government, spiritual, scientific, and educational activity throughout Egypt because the temples themselves are the books, encyclopedias and libraries of Ancient times. With this accumulated knowledge and wisdom, the Ancient Egyptians civilized the entire world.

Papyrus is the world's first form of paper, also it played a critical part in the development and dissemination of the Ancient Egyptian culture in the form of scrolls.

A papyrus is a water plant that grows in the Nile River. The plant is steeped in symbolism; Ancient Egyptians used the fiber of its stem as writing material. Its stem grows from 3 to 10 feet in height, the stem of a papyrus is triangular, symbolically representing a pyramid, and its sharp edged leaves form a spherical scope, symbolic of the Sun.

The stems of these plants are peeled and sliced into thin strips, they are soaked to relieve them of sugar, and then they are laid horizontally side by side. Another layer is applied vertically in the same manner, both sides are covered with cloth to which pressure is applied for six days. Papyrus was the first form of paper, it provided a convenient way for the Ancient Egyptians to transport their knowledge worldwide. Although the Ancient Egyptians are the most studied culture in history, questions constantly arise as to the race of these multi-social, political, spiritual, and scientific geniuses.

The Ancient Egyptians passionately proclaimed themselves, through their self-portraits etched in stone and carved in mountains throughout the temples and pyramids of Egypt, as an African people. The Ancient Egyptians and their descendants, who now call themselves African-Americans, Blacks, Negroes, Nubians, Sudanese, Ethiopians etc., created and developed animal husbandry, agriculture, cosmetics, internal medicine and mortuary science, the calendar and the world's first true democracy. These are the people who created the natural sciences, mathematics, architecture, civil, and mechanical engineering. The monuments and inventions of Ancient Egypt collectively embody all disciplines previously mentioned, and are the foundation for all modern scientific development and research. They employed mathematical and scientific principles yet to be rediscovered; for many of these awesome structures, and inventions have not been duplicated, even with today's technology. Let it not be misunderstood, Dr. Walter Williams has propounded that the Ancient Egyptians invented writing and the world's first three alphabets; the hieroglyphic, hieratic, and phonetic scripts. Every alphabet used in the world today is based on one of these three alphabets created by the Ancient Egyptians. These claims are documented and justified by the fruits of their labor, which stand today as a testament to their greatness which are validated by the previously discussed monuments and structures.

These great technological feats are just half of the equation that constitutes the creators of civilization. The other half is their commitment to humanity and spirituality. Since the inception of the Ancient Egyptian civilization, the people of Egypt incorporated what is known as the Maatian Creed in every aspect of their lives. This creed encompasses the concepts of peace, love, wisdom, truth and justice. Unlike European cultures that later obtained relatively higher levels of technological advancement through assimilation, the Ancient Egyptians never oppressed the people they visited, to the contrary, they elevated the people they visited with respect for their culture. This is evidenced by the people of India, China, Central America, and North America, their civilizations started at the point in time of their contact with the Ancient Egyptians.

Spiritual Systems, Religions, Systems of Government and the Sun

Spiritual systems are not to be confused with religions. Traditionally, spiritual systems were native to the region where they were created. It is for this reason spiritual systems do not have names. They are intertwined and inseparable from the traditions, customs, rules, and laws that formulate the nature of the society where they were developed. Whether the term was oracle, sage, elder, wise man, doctor, witch doctor, monk, prophet, or priest they all were part of the same legacy of individuals who first initiated the study of nature, or individuals later trained by their society to be keepers, preservers and transmitters of this critical knowledge. These individuals formed councils, and in many instances, elected one from their ranks to be the eminent leader of their communities Historically, spiritual systems were not excessively concerned with an individual's personal relationship with their creator. Spiritual systems were uniquely concerned with the social and political development of the entire community as well as the development of codes of conduct , from which a systematic and fair resolution of conflicts was mandated. There was no competition between rival spiritual systems because initially each culture had only one spiritual system. Traditionally, when a person was born into a native culture, they were born into the spiritual system of that culture. On the other hand, religions today are imported, synthetic, and unnatural. In most cases they are not native to the society who practice them, they all have names because they are foreign to the societies receiving them, and one needs to distinguish them from the native spiritual system or other implanted religions. Today's religions are allegories deceptively made real in the minds of their believers. Originally, the concept of religion was not concerned with the supernatural, deception, or mind control. Initially, the term religion was derived from the term to venerate, to make holy and to set aside. This ultimately equated to the gathering and preservation of critical solar knowledge, and laws of nature. Which, in order to achieve the stability necessary for advancement, to become a civilized society, any developing culture would have to be aware.

A state of order and a sense of right and wrong are the prerequisites for civil living, yet in modern day thought, they are indelibly tied to Western religions. Religions did not precede morality, it existed long before man created religion. Morality did not start with the Western religions including Christianity, Islam, or Judaism. Morality was in part precluded with the advent of Western religions.

Prior to the "European Renaissance" the Catholic Church sold indulgences to its parishioners as a means to increase its treasury, and as a way for noblemen to buy forgiveness for their injury to other people. According to Christian doctrine, one does not receive the rewards of afterlife by doing good deeds or by being fair and honest. One could be the greatest liar, thief, or murderer that ever lived and need only accept Christianity and "Jesus the Christ" as their personal savior to be forgiven and saved. In the Jewish religion, the faithful ask for atonement or forgiveness before they plan and commit their wrongdoing "sins" for the coming year. In both cases there is little or no regard for morality. These religions provide those who fully understand their underlying principles a license to prey on the unsuspecting.

Morality, normally, is a natural outgrowth of a society's spiritual system. Even in their most idealistic state, religions claim to be a compilation of ethics which regulate interpersonal actions. However, in actuality, religions are in many cases politically organized systems manipulated to control the people by having them disregard their innate intellect and instincts and replace them with "faith" or unquestioned belief. Because religions carry a political intent, they are forced on the population of a particular region through deceptive theory, and even physical violence.

Coming Forth By Day

The Ancient Egyptians Funeral text is a compilation of writing describing the entrance and journey into the afterworld of the deceased. It describes the Ancient Egyptians creation stories where the heart of the deceased is weighted on the scale of justice. Counterweight to a feather representing Maat (truth, peace, love and justice). If during the life of the deceased their wrong deeds out number their good deeds, the deceased heart would outweigh the feather, which symbolizes that the deceased would never see the Afterworld .

However, there was an alternate way to enter the Afterworld, and this path involves entering the Hall of Justice. This is where the forty two judges reside and where one declares their righteousness by reciting the forty two negative confessions, which is also the conceptual source of the biblical Ten Commandments. Here are fifteen examples of the forty two negative confessions

1. I have not done iniquity.
2. I have not robbed with violence.
3. I have not stolen.
4. I have done no murder; I have done no harm.
5. I have not defrauded offerings.
6. I have not diminished obligations.
7. I have not plundered the Nether.
8. I have not spoken lies.
9. I have not snatched away food.
10. I have not caused pain.
11. I have not committed fornication.
12. I have not caused shedding of tears.
13. I have not dealt deceitfully.
14. I have not transgressed.
15. I have not acted guilefully.

These writings are a composite of writings primarily found on the walls of pyramids and carved on coffins, respectively known as the pyramid and coffin text; additionally, these writings are also found on

Tomb Stelae (gravestone) and in the subterranean burial chambers of the Valley of the Kings. Today these writings are known as THE ANCIENT EGYPTIANS BOOK OF THE DEAD. The Book of the Dead is deemed the source of the Ancient Egyptian creation stories. A part of these writings are long flowing scenic paintings depicting critical detail from the Ancient Egyptians creation stories such as the Judgments Hall, the scale of justice and the cyclical relationship between Nut (the sky), Ra (the Sun) and Ihy the (Sun of the Sun) and Hathor (the holy cow or holy mother). These scenes literally put these depictions of the creation stories in motion and are tantamount to a motion picture... Western academia has confined the relevance of these documents to the moral code of the Ancient Egyptians; Ra (the Sun).

The Ancient Egyptians Creation Stories, and the Sun

The Ancient Egyptians Spiritual System is a symbolic embodiment of the principles and laws of physical science, as they relate to the control of the natural forces on Earth. These nature forces are personified as deities who take human form. The foundation for the Ancient Egyptians Spiritual System is contained within their creation story known as the Ennead. The Ennead is an allegory based upon nature. The Ancient Egyptians based their governmental, spiritual, and social systems on the concepts contained in this story. The Ennead literally means nine deities. The first five deities pertain to creation, and the last four deities pertain to mankind and nature. This story is portrayed on three levels; astronomical, geological, and sociological. In explaining the laws of nature, the various natural forces on Earth are depicted as deities. These deities (forces) attributes are equated with those of animals or natural occurrences thought to highlight or display certain characteristics. In this system of deities and natural forces, the Sun, which exists on the astronomical plane, is regarded as the creator, the "Giver of Life." The validation of this idea is encompassed in the fact that life could not exist on Earth without the Sun. The Sun's first set of offspring is Ma at and Shu, who are female and male, representing moisture and air respectively. Through the creator, Maat and Shu gave birth to Nut and Geb. Nut represents the sky and atmosphere, and Geb represents the Earth. Nut was born on top of Geb. Shu separates the sky, Nut, from the Earth, Geb and in many depictions of Nut in funeral text, Nut swallows the Sun in the evening and for twelve hours or through the 12 divisions of the underworld that the Sun travels through when in Nuts body during the night. The Sun is reborn every day at Sunrise symbolizing the resurrection of the administrator. On a geological level, Nut and Geb gave birth to the four deities who actually live on Earth and have human characteristics. Horus "The son of the Sun," Isis (Aset), Seth, and Nephthys together connect the natural forces with that of human nature.

Horus has astronomical aspects as well as a sociological heritage. Horus is depicted as a falcon, falcons are birds of prey which fly extremely high, therefore falcons are closely associated with Horus and Horus is closely associated with the Sun and the sky. Falcons are also known for their keen sight. The eye of Horus or the falcon is the embodiment of both the light of the Sun and insight of those who observe the consequences of the Earth's orbit of the Sun. Astronomically, Horus is one with Ihy, who was the offspring of Ra (the Sun) and Nut (the sky). After Nut gave birth to Ihy (THE Moon)"The Sun of the Sun," she becomes known as Hathor "The Cow, Mother." Horus and Seth, males, were born as twins. Horus, being the eldest, represents good, and Seth represents evil. Horus, being the eldest was given dominion over Egypt. Seth became jealous, and subsequently killed Horus and cuts his body into fourteen pieces. Seth buried his body parts throughout Egypt, then disposed of his penis, by throwing it into the Nile where consumed by a fish. Isis (Aset) and Nephthys, females, were also born as twins. Isis (Aset) and Nephthys traveled throughout Egypt and reclaimed Horus' body parts, with the exception of the penis, they reassembled his body with the help of Thoth and wrapped him up as a mummy, thus causing him to be renamed Osiris (Ausara) in death. Horus/ Ihy, eventually reproduced himself in the body of his sister Isis (Aset) producing the first Immaculate Conception and establishing order and justice.

The Memphite Theology has been designated the original creation story emanating from Ancient Egypt. It was supposedly discovered in Memphis Egypt. Memphis, the capital of Ancient Egypt during the time of antiquity is where Upper and Lower Egypt were unified to become the world's first nation. However, after close examination, the Memphite theology is exposed as a variation of the Ennead. Its development is different, but the final composition is the same as the Ennead except for the addition of Ptah-Ta-Tjenen who superseded RA or Atum as the

Creator. The Memphite Theology states that in the beginning there was chaos. Out of this ocean of chaotic confusion emerged the Primeval Hill which is symbolically represented by a pyramid and an obelisk, this hill is ultimately equated to the establishment of world order.

With the death of Horus-Osiris (Ausara), Geb acting as arbiter, rescinded his Original order which divided Egypt between Horus and Seth and gave all of Egypt to Horus'/Osiris (Ausara)' firstborn, Horus Jr. This action brought order to Ancient Egypt.

Upon analysis of the Memphite Theology, it becomes apparent that the Memphite Theology came about as a result of the death of an Egyptian Governor; this death caused disorder and confusion as to who would govern Ancient Egypt. The town of Memphis was born out of this chaos and discord. The Memphite Theology is purely a political doctrine whose purpose was to formulate a process of succession that would assure both a smooth and orderly transfer of authority. Memphis was established amid Lower and Upper Egypt as a compromise between the temple system and priest societies of Lower and Upper Egypt. These priest societies are symbolized within the Memphite Theology as the Ennead itself (that council of deities who represent discord and order).

The Ancient Egyptians used the scarab or dung beetle as a symbol to represent the Primeval Hill, primarily because these insects emerged from the fertile soil of the inundated Nile River in the same manner that Memphis was said to have emerged from the chaos described in the Memphite Theology. Scarabs are known for taking cow dung and fashioning it into a round shaped object which symbolizes the Sun moving across the sky. The Ancient Egyptians recognized the fertilizing power inherent with animal dung, and for that reason the Ancient Egyptians associated the Sun or Ra with this dung that scarabs rolled as the life giving force that is characteristic of both subjects. Scarabs were also identified with Ptah the Creator. (p.138B, p.135C) The Ancient Egyptians considered the Nile River another source of life giving energy, because it was the source for water and fertilized soil to the arid Nile Valley. For the Ancient Egyptians, the Sun and fertile Nile were critical to the maintenance of life giving vegetation and to creating a greenhouse effect.

Throughout this whole process the spiritual manifestation of the creator is in balance with the establishment of female and male deities who compliment and assist each other in bringing forth the foundation of the spiritual system of the Ancient Egyptians in the form of a symbolic cosmic system of order. Although the Ancient Egyptians had a myriad of deities, it must be understood that these deities were symbolic manifestations of the various characteristics assigned to the Creator.

The term monotheism denotes the belief in one god. In Western society this practice is held with much esteem. Primarily because the developer of monotheism is believed to be the creator of civilization. The incarnated non historical biblical Jew is given credit for this concept. However, to give them creditability, these false people must be connected with a real people, the Ancient Egyptians. Therefore a so called Semitic group, known as the Hyksos, was invented and fictitiously placed in Ancient Egypt as invaders. In his many lectures over the years Dr. Walter Williams was the first to establish the Hyksos as an invented people, used to create a Jew in human form. These false invaders are given credit for introducing the Ancient Egyptians to monotheism. However, monotheism was not initially adopted during the 16th dynasty as the Western academicians would like the world to believe.

There is no credible evidence of a Hyksos existence, where did the Hyksos come from? Where is the Archeological evidence, of the Hyksos in Egypt? The invading Greeks had a homeland. The Ancient invading Romans had a homeland. The Ancient invading Libyans had a homeland. Where is the homeland of the Hyksos? How can a foreign people take over a complete nation without a supply line trailing back to their homeland?

As conquering invaders the Greek and Roman and the Ancient Egyptians neighboring brother the Nubians sat on the throne of Isis (Aset) as Rulers and Governor of Ancient Egypt respectively. Where are the Hyksos as ruler of Egypt? The Western writer of Ancient history has been given a pass to magically make the Hyksos appear and disappear with their pens whenever and however it is convenient to maintain the lie and try to establish a non-historic Semite or Jew in the form of a Hyksos in Egypt during this time. Logically, this pen can only represent wishful thinking and mental illusion and not real physical archeological evidence.

A re-emphasis may have been placed on the Sun disk (The Creator) during this period rather than the attributes of the other entities of the Ennead. Monotheism had its origin at the inception of the Ancient Egyptian civilization.

The Ancient Egyptians creation stories the Ennead and the Memphite Theology serve as the Ancient Egyptians Constitution. Here lies the foundation and the basis of the Ancient Egyptians Educational (scientific), spiritual, governmental and social developments all embedded in one institution. This constitution symbolically established the Sun (RA) as the one and only creator, and with this one act and acknowledgment monotheism is instituted for the first time. The Ancient Egyptians developed the first spiritual system and monotheism was an inherent part of that system. Just as the Ancient Egyptians creator can be dissolved into multiple principles (the Ancient Egyptians divine Trinity and Ennead) so can the Christian model (the Christian divine Trinity).

The Ancient Egyptians Cosmology and The Sun

In modern Western thought, astronomy and astrology are looked upon as similar yet different views of the cosmos, even though their foundation is practically the same. Astrology is looked upon as a belief and Astronomy as a science. Astrology is confined primarily to the Solar system, while Astronomy is used to define the limits of the universe. However, there is an ironic twist and unsuspected exchange of roles. In the Western world the Solar system, is a subject that is supposed to be well known to Academia. However, many of its attributes cannot be proven to have direct or indirect impact on the various meteorological systems of Earth. This fact has given rise to theories merged with lies and myths that have relegated astrology to a cult-like belief. Simultaneously, the galaxies and astronomy have the same problem as the solar system, only more flawed because of extreme distances.

Astrology is based on the so called precession of the Equinoxes and Stellar constellations. Theoretically, the precession of the Equinoxes is the force which drives the dawning of a new age. An Astrological age is based on theological philosophy and is determined by the constellation in which the Sun rises during the vernal equinox. Also constellations are the foundation of astrology. They are distinct star groupings which when graphically linked are characterized as humans and animals. They can be characterized as depicting natural phenomenons such as Aquarius the water bearer, Taurus the bull, Leo the lion, Virgo the Virgin, Aries the ram, Cancer the crab, Gemini the twin, Capricorn the goat, Libra the scales of justice, Scorpio the scorpion, Sagittarius the archer man and Pisces the fish. The Zodiacal constellations are those star groupings which appear on the eastern horizon and are associated with a particular month of the year. The constellation which is visible during the Equinox is thought to change counterclockwise every 2160 years, and the reason for this idea is that the Sun is thought to revolve around the center of the Galaxy every 25000 years. However, during the course of the Earth's orbit of the Sun, the Sun rises clockwise in a different zodiacal constellation every month. As a result, certain constellations are associated with particular planets. These planets are visible within those constellations.

Many European scholars have made Sirius the "Dog Star" the prominent determinant for the start of the Ancient Egyptian year partially because the Nile's annual inundation coincides with the appearance of Sirius. With the exception of the Sun, Sirius is the brightest star in the sky. During the period between July and August Sirius rises and sets with the Sun. This period is known as the Dog Days of summer because it is hot and uncomfortable. Although there is a school of thought emanating from Western academia which claims that the Ancient Egyptians went through a Stellar phase before going through a Solar phase. I find this line of thought to be absurd. The Stellar phase was not only subordinate to the Solar phase, it was secondary to the lunar phase and was a much later development. The Stellar phase was not the conceptual principle that established the time concept, because it is far too abstract to be a founding principle. Other than navigational purposes such as long distance travel, tracking planets, illuminating the sky after dark and a further refinement of time of year, there are few other tangible or concrete benefits in studying stars.

A popular science fiction space television series in the Sixties developed a large and devoted following. This series is based on the imaginary travel of mutant characters into deep space. We must remember that the Sun is considered a star; consequently, in ancient times and now star tracking, actually entails what seems to be the detailed tracking of the Sun across the sky. The Sun was the key then and it is the key now. This study was not only practical, it also set the parameters for modern and Ancient civilizations.

Many of our scholars report or mimic the misinterpretation of what is called the Zodiac of Dendera and the Ancient Egyptian calendar. Instead of analyzing and studying the consequences of which such absurd projections would yield, they accept these projections without reservation.

The only way that anyone can have a true understanding of Ancient Egypt and ancient history is to do like the Ancient Egyptians, follow the dictates of nature. The Zodiac of Dendera confers two powerful tenets which overtly follow this criteria. 1. A zodiac calendar based on twelve months and 2. A year divided into four principle sections. Unfortunately, modern interpretation of this symbolic table is confused. Based on a further interpretation of the Zodiac of Dendera, European scholars state that the Ancient Egyptians recognized only three seasons, consisting of four months each. Each month consists of 30 days, subdivided into three weeks, each consisting of 10 days. The Zodiac of Dendera is a circular plate which was discovered at the temple in Dendera Egypt. Shortly after the discovery it was stolen and moved to Paris, France. On the outer dimension of the Zodiac of Dendera there is a procession of 36 figures. These figures are called decants and they are said to represent the rising of the constellations every ten days. It is from these 36 decants or gods that the European scholars based their assumption that the Ancient Egyptian calendar and year was based on 36 weeks. However, it must be mentioned that graphically this plate is symmetrically divided into four major sections representing the four seasons. There is a further subdivision of each season into three months. However , the symmetry ends there.

These decants which are thought to represent weeks are not evenly divided into each month. Nor, does each month contain three decants. Some months only have one decant where others have as many as five decants. Therefore, these figures could not have been used to represent the week concept. Clearly, this calendar is not establishing a week concept based on the 36 decants, but simply representing the 36 zodiac decants as they present themselves during the natural year.

But probably the most outlandish claim which was accepted without question or challenge was this claim which states in the year 4241 B.C.E. the Ancient Egyptians created a calendar that was adjusted every 1460 years with the addition of an extra year. This supposedly was to compensate for the 5 hours 48 minutes and 46 seconds beyond the 365 days that it takes the Earth to complete its annual cycle around the Sun. But with some basic logic and simple math this notion becomes another miscue. The Ancient Egyptians are said to have used the Earth year as the foundation for their calendar. A Earth year is a period which extends from Vernal Equinox to Vernal Equinox. The Ancient Egyptians would not spend 1460 years to bring the Earth year into alignment with this calendar and still fall short of the natural year by 11 2/5 days. Yet this is the consequence of this projection.

By breaking down the 5 hours 48 minutes and 46 seconds into seconds, which gives you 20926 seconds, then by multiplying these seconds by 1460, the number of years that it was stated that the Ancient Egyptians waited before they added an extra year to their calendar brings this figure to equal 30,551,960 seconds. When we divide this figure 30,551,960 seconds by 86400 seconds the number of seconds within a day, you will come up with 353.61 days instead of 365.2591 days. Moreover, above and beyond this claim, I find it astonishing that this claim can be made without anyone challenging it. A situation like the one just mentioned goes against every fundamental Solar principle that the Ancient Egyptians established. This illogical solution would not only disrupt the anticipation of the four GEO/SOLAR OCCURRENCES and the four seasons, it would also unduly corrupt every year for the next 1456 years.

If the previous theory were correct, approximately every four years the Ancient Egyptian year, based on this calendar, would have advanced by a day eventually destroying the predictability in the seasons and the weather pattern. Given this theory, fall would eventually come when it was actually spring, summer and winter. Winter would eventually come when it was actually spring, summer and fall. Spring would ultimately come in summer, fall and winter. Summer would ultimately come during spring, fall and winter. Thereby negating the main reason for a time concept or calendar. Without a consistent time concept there is no definitive pattern. Without a definitive time concept there are no guiding principles, no structure, only confusion, anarchy and barbarism. A state of existence which is diametrically opposed to the Ancient Egyptians legacy.

In ancient times a partial or total eclipse probably caused periods of uncertainty and/or fear. To the untrained eye a solar eclipse may seem to be unexplainable and occur sporadically. A solar eclipse occurs when the Sun, the Moon and the Earth are all in alignment. The Moon temporarily blocks Sunlight from the Earth. A solar eclipse only occurs during the day and only when the Moon is in its new Moon phase, the Earth temporarily blocks Sunlight from the Moon. In a Solar eclipse the Moon causes the sky to darken during the day which can cause a reduction in the temperature. The lunar eclipse occurs when the Sun, the Moon and the Earth are in alignment. A lunar eclipse only occurs at night and only when the Moon is in its Full Moon phase, during this time the Moon appears to be blue. Therefore anyone with this knowledge probably would be looked upon as a forecaster and wise man, someone who could possibly foresee the future and serve as a leader of the community. Even though eclipses are global events, at most an eclipse lasts no more than seven minutes, and the effected areas are regional. Eclipses are cyclical and therefore can be forecast in every 18 year and 11 day cycle known as Saros. This period represents 223 lunations and a lunation represents 29.53 days or a lunar cycle. The Saros cycle reoccurs every 6585.32 days but shifts in longitude 120 degrees farther west creating a three Saros cycle in which the eclipses reoccur in the exact same location every 54 years and 34 days. The Saros cycle is a powerful natural principle which links the hidden Ancient Egyptians Lunar month calendar to the Ancient Egyptian Solar time system. The Saros cycle also acts as both the prelude to and foundation of the Metonic cycles. The Metonic cycles are used to connect Western religions to the Ancient Egyptian time system.

Other interesting Astronomical events that can be seen from Earth are the Mercury and Venus transit.

The Venus transit is a phenomenon that occurs cyclically twice in a one hundred and eight year period. The Mercury transit occurs around twenty times a Century. Mercury, Venus and Earth are considered inner planets. Mercury, Venus and Earth in the order listed are the closest Planets to the Sun. From Earth only the two most inner planets Mercury and Venus appear to travel cross the Sun's Surface. These occurrences are known as the Mercury transit and the Venus transit. These occurrences happen when the Sun, Mercury or Venus and the Earth are in alignment.

These illusions are quite impressive because both Mercury and Venus seem to make their transit from one end of what appears to be a Solar Disk to the other end of the Solar Disk in less than an Earth day (24 hours).

The Mercury and Venus transit look as if they cover half or 50% of the circumference of their orbit of the Sun, because they seem to travel completely across the surface. However, if the stated length of Mercury's orbit of the Sun is correct as 88 Earth days and if the stated length of

Venus's orbit of the Sun is correct as 241 Earth days, then what we are witnessing in the case of the Mercury transit is not a distance that is 50% of its circumference of its orbit of the Sun but a distance that is less than 1.13% of the circumference of its orbit of the Sun. In the case of Venus transit you are not witnessing a distance that is 50% of its circumference of its orbit of the Sun but a distance that is less than .41% of the circumference of its orbit of the Sun. Because the Sun, Earth, Venus and Mercury are all sphere shaped objects their movement with respect to each other is angular and presents a view that in its totality is abstract from that which is actually occurring.

The Earth's Orbit of the Sun and the Development of a Time Concept

The Sun and the Moon are the only Astrological bodies that can be proven to have a significant effect on the environments of the Earth. Influences from any other bodies in the Solar system, galaxies or universe are only speculative and cannot be proven. The Sun, is considered a star. A star is a self-luminous celestial object which sends heat, light and energy in all directions. The Sun is the only star that is known to have natural satellites. Of which the Earth is one of nine known planets. A natural satellite is a smaller celestial body that revolves around a larger host celestial body. Several planets are acknowledged to have natural satellites; the Earth is known to have one, the Moon.

Note: *There is a subclass of Astronomical bodies found in the Solar system known as asteroids, meteorites and comets; these bodies may periodically have some minor effects on the environment of the Earth. Asteroids are secondary or miniature planets which revolve around the Sun like the Earth, Mars and Saturn. They are found basically between Mars and Jupiter. This area is known as the Asteroid belt. Planets that are found between the Sun and the Asteroid belt Venus, Mercury Earth and Mars are called inner planets. Planets found outside of the Asteroid belt Jupiter, Saturn, Uranus, Neptune and Pluto are known as the Outer Planets. More than 30,000 asteroids are known to exist. The largest one called Ceres, is about 600 miles in diameter. Colliding asteroids are thought to be the source of meteorites. Meteorites are Astronomical bodies which actually strike or collide with the Earth. In most instances* *the Earth's atmosphere causes them to disintegrate before they hit the surface. However, it has been theorized that some larger meteorites, which survive the Earth's atmosphere can cause a catastrophic explosion when they hit the Earth's surface. This would undoubtedly cause a disaster locally, and possibly cause small changes in the atmosphere and weather regionally and globally. Comets, may possibly affect the Earth's environment because their multi-annual orbit periodically brings them close enough to Earth to have some type of gravitational effect. Comets orbit the Sun in a route which crosses and/or intersects the orbits of other planets.*

The Geo/Solar Occurrences are the best and easiest method for determining the time of year. This method is location specific, meaning, that if you change your location you would need to set up a new template for the solar markers.

The Sun rises in the East and sets in the West. Along the eastern horizon for 182 days the Sun rises from different spots advancing the Sun from low in the South East until it appears high in the North East. On the 183rd day for the next 179 days the Sun starts its march back from high in the North East to low into South East. Solar markers can be created and set at the low, middle and high points, representing the December Solstice, The Equinoxes and June Solstice encircling the entire year approximately 91 days, between each marker. When the Sun parallels key Sun markers that can denote the start of a new season.

Between the Sun, Earth and the Moon, our concept of time is established. The Earth, the Sun and the Moon together form an Astronomical clock and calendar. This system served as the timepiece of antiquity and it is the ultimate timepiece today. (p.45 A) At mans' most fundamental level, the concept of time regulates our sleeping and our biological clock with the daily rising and setting of the Sun. On an individual level time is used to gauge a person or group's development from childhood to adolescence, from adolescence to adulthood, from adulthood to an elder. Through the duration of time an infant developmental milestone can be a more critical gauge. Each stage in human development carries with it a certain set of expectations and/or responsibilities.

A concept of time is also essential in establishing a stable community. With a concept of time a people will eventually stop migrating from place to place in search of food. With a concept of time a community can see things in cycles, a community can also predict the changes in seasons, forecast weather patterns and foresee animal migrations. With a concept of time, a community can regulate planting and harvesting seasons. A time concept also allows a people to predict low and high tides on the water ways, all with a high degree of accuracy.

Take the following example. Because the menstrual cycle of most non-pregnant women closely coincides with the number of days it takes the Moon to orbit the Earth, the Moon can be used as a cursor or marker to help predict and regulate not only personal hygiene, but human birth, and other biological births, such as farm animals. Using the various phases of the Moon, the Moon can be used to determine when a non-pregnant woman can conceive or if the woman is pregnant. The Moon can also be used to predict the expected day of birth. The menstrual cycle of women whose ages fall within the child bearing years is approximately 28 days. This period compares favorably with the orbital cycle of the Moon which is around 29½ days. Constants are established and these constants become the foundation for the social organization of a society.

The Ancient Egyptians very early in their development studied the Sun and the Moon, then by way of observation and correlation deduced principles and laws from those studies. Astronomy and astrology should not be seen as opposing disciplines for they are in reality one discipline. Astronomy is considered the scientific study of the universe beyond the Earth. Astrology is the study of this same region, but with the belief that the stars and planets have a direct influence on the daily course of one's life. For the Ancient Egyptians, the principles that comprise Astronomy provided the foundation for the establishment of time.

However, beyond the superficial connotations of astrology today, historically Astrology was created as a notational system which provided and assigned a graphic symbol to specify a period of time depicting the relative position of the Earth in it's annual orbit around the Sun. Within a year, the Moon orbits the Earth 12 times. A lunar cycle is equal to a natural month, and a month is equal to a zodiac sign. The Earth lunar system is a cursory system. It naturally indicates important predictable information about the Earth's environment, based on its current number of orbits around the Earth within a year. Natural cycles are the rudiments of time because they provide consistent points of reference. Without recurring, predictable natural cycles there can be no time concept.

What is regarded as noon is the meridian of the natural day. In the temperate and tropic zones noon occurs daily when the Sun reaches its highest point in the sky. It naturally divides the day into two sections, each section containing an equal amount of daylight and darkness.

A New Moon or Lunar Cycle occurs approximately every 29.5 days, the lunar cycle officially starts with the new Moon. During this period the Moon is not visible.

Everyday the Moon presents a different face to the Earth. For 29 and a half days this changing face can be calculated and gauged. Shortly after a New Moon a crescent Moon appears, the crescent Moon continues to wax or build for approximately thirteen days subsequently establishing a full Moon on the fifteenth day. The full Moon wanes or diminishes for fourteen days until it completely disappears and completes the lunar cycle. With the end of the old lunar cycle comes the start of a New Moon. A crescent Moon occurs just before and right after the New Moon and new month. The waxing crescent has a concave edge while the waning crescent has a convex edge. (p.42B)

A day represents the time that it takes the Earth to complete one revolution on it axis. A natural month is symbolic of the period it takes the Moon to complete its orbit of the Earth. The start of a season is a checkpoint or milestone in the Earth's orbit of the Sun. It denotes a significant change in the weather and the amount of Sunlight within a day. A year denotes the period it takes the Earth to complete its orbit around the Sun.

Just as a day, month, season and year has a natural genesis, so does a week. The start of a Moon phase is the official start of the week. Inherent in a lunar based calendar the start of a new year will not always start at the beginning of the lunar cycle. Thereby making necessary the concept of the week to approximate the start of the month even though the Moon or month may have aged beyond the new Moon phase. Encompassed within the natural lunar cycle are the four distinctive phases or periods which can be used to represent the start of the lunar cycle and year, thereby making the beginning week or phase of a new year and new month relative to the start of the New Year. At this point a logical or relative month or Moon comes in play. These months can start with a first quarter and end with the first quarter, they can start with the full Moon and end with the full Moon, or start with the last quarter and end with the last quarter.

A natural month can be subdivided into natural weeks, each averaging 7.3826 days per week and quantified by seven or eight days. (p.42A) Randomly within the period of two natural months (59 days) five of the eight weeks within this period would include 7 days while the remaining 3 weeks would contain 8 days. The start of the first, second, third and fourth week of a natural month can be represented by any of the four phases of the Moon : the new Moon , the half Moon , the full Moon and the old Moon. The half Moon is synonymous with the first quarter of the Moon and the old Moon is synonymous with the last quarter of the Moon.

Week#	Starting Phase	Ending Phase
1	new Moon -	first quarter
2	first quarter -	full Moon
3	full Moon -	last quarter
4	last quarter -	new Moon

By gazing up any day of the month you can tell what week you are in by studying the phase of the Moon. In the current example the first week of a new Moon or natural month starts with the new Moon and ends with the first quarter. The second week starts on the first quarter and ends with the full Moon. The third week of a natural month starts with a full Moon and ends with the last quarter. And the forth week of a natural month starts with the last quarter and ends with the new Moon. A week concept based on anything other than a 7.3826 day week has no practical purpose. (p.43)

If a week did not denote a Moon phase what would be it's purpose? What would be the significance of a 5 day week, 10 day week or a 12 day week? What natural event occurs every five, ten, or twelve days which would denote a natural week? None. Originally a week had only one purpose, and that was to denote a particular period of time based on the phases of the Moon. In Western society the week concept lost it's correlation with the lunar cycle, but it still retains vestiges of it's original purpose in paying homage to the Sun every seven days and by subdividing the month into four parts. The first day of a Moon phase represented the start of the week and is actually a reflection and celebration of the Sun.

The concept of a Blue Moon has been the subject of many songs and poems. It is defined as a full Moon occurring twice within a calendar month, once at the beginning and again at the end of the month. However, the Western world's historical and scientific communities have systematically diverted the entire world away from a factual understanding of the actual length of the natural month by claiming that the Ancient Egyptians based their month on a thirty day period. Then the astronomers claim that both the Moon's day and the Moon's orbit of the Earth is based on a 27.333 day cycle with reference to a fixed star. Then these same astronomers contradict this claim when they state that the lunar day and lunar night both equals approximately 15 days which would produce a lunar cycle of 29.5 days, the true length of the lunar cycle in reference to the Sun. Because, the lunar cycle is 29.5 days, at least one of the full Moons that occur during a Blue Moon would occur during the day. When the Moon appears during the day it appears the same color as the sky, blue, hence the term, blue Moon.

The term pagan is defined as relating to ancient religion or relating to an ancient religion that had many gods and praised nature. The whole concept of paganism is antithetical to what is true, real and legitimate. Ironically the deliberate offensive nature of the term is designed to dissolve the connection this concept has with Western religions. Naturalism is the practice of the Ancient Egyptians, transmitted through their creation stories in the form of symbolism and parable. Paganism, at its foundation is a modified form of naturalism practiced by the Greek and Romans and is the mother of Western religion in general and Christianity in particular. Paganism is not the opposite of Western religion. Paganism is at the heart of Western Religion.

Animist is another nature based belief system which states that the creative life force exists in all things. Because all things on Earth are derived from the creator, every object or thing must be respected, and not taken for granted, the creator is everywhere at the same time. Within the Animist philosophy is a theme that dictates conservation in the consumption of natural resources, take only what's needed, no more and no less. This policy restricts waste and promotes thriftiness.

Western Religions and The Earth's Orbit of the Sun

To further illustrate the importance of planetary movement, especially as it relates to the development of a concept of time and the establishment of the Ancient Egyptians knowledge base, let's examine the deployment of the first man-made religion, Christianity, as a political operative. Note that many of the concepts that were not applied to Christianity were later adapted to Islam and Judaism.

The foundation of Christianity is based on the concepts within Ancient Egyptian spiritual system. Principles such as the judgment, the immaculate conception, The Thanksgiving, The Crucifixion/Killing, The Resurrection and the divine triad provided the basic tenets used in Christianity thousands of years before Christianity was developed. Many more precepts and concepts came about as a result of the Coptic Egyptians under the duress of the Greeks and Romans. The Greek speaking Coptic Egyptian, were forced to fashion for their Greek overlords a pseudo Spiritual system by creating a human inspired and man manufactured religion called Christianity. This was done by formulating principles and rules in the form of the Eucharist and the Nicene Homoousios Reform Creed. Yet, above and beyond the fact that there was a historical process which eventually developed into Christianity, one fact remains constant and that fact is a historical Jesus the Christ, as it pertains to biblical account, is an incarnated character that never existed in real life. See Dr. Walter Williams' Historical Origin of Christianity. This powerful fact not only invalidates the Central Object of Christianity, it also invalidates Christianity itself along with all of its supporting characters.

Christianity has two critical holidays (Christmas and Easter). These holidays are more closely related to their Ancient Egyptian origin rather than their manufactured supposed fictional origin. According to today's Christian theology, Easter is a festival in the Christian religion celebrating the resurrection of Jesus the Christ. This holiday is held on the first Sunday after the date of the first full Moon which occurs after March 20 (the vernal equinox).

Christmas, is a day that is celebrated to honor the birthday of the created Jesus the Christ. The twelve days of Christmas occur from December 26 thru January 6, the days the fictitious three Wise Men visited the Christ child. Jesus the Christ is supposedly the son of God, sent to Earth to save mankind from sin. While on Earth, as the story goes, he was crucified on the day now known as Good Friday. Two days after his (supposed) crucifixion (Easter Sunday), he rose from the dead and ascended into heaven. If Easter had no relationship with Ancient Egypt, then why isn't the so called resurrection celebrated on the day that it supposedly happened, rather than tied directly to the vernal equinox which occurs around March 20.

Easter and Passover can be explained on two additional levels beyond their perverted biblical account. The first level pertains to the meshing of the Gregorian and 'Jewish' calendars.

Easter is actually an amalgamation of natural principles with the superficial ideas, because Easter incorporates myths and lies with principles of nature. As mentioned earlier the historical foundation for Easter is derived from an Ancient Egyptian festival celebrating the start of spring. This is signified by the vernal equinox. But after understanding this principle concept other adjunct questions arise.

For instance, why is it that the date for Easter must be calculated every year and why is it that this holiday must come on a Sunday, on or after a full Moon. According to biblical literature the incarnated "Christ" was celebrating Passover before he was arrested and crucified. Passover is a contrived holiday, along with fictitious characters, that is associated with the biblical "Hebrews or Jews". The Jewish calendar is pre-dated, It was created and maintained to bring validation to the stories in Old Testament bible literature.

As the story goes Passover takes place in the "Jewish" month Nisan. Passover comes from the biblical story of the Ten Plagues in Exodus, a book of the Old Testament; although the Ten Commandments should be the climactic part of the Exodus, it is actually anti-climactic and its treatment purely secondary. The so called ten laws of Moses is just an afterthought to the ten plagues which tries to connect the incarnated "Jews" to the Ancient Egyptians. The God of the "Jews" issued the ten plagues against the Egyptians to force them to free the "Jews" and as punishment for holding the "Jews" in bondage. These plagues took the following form:

1. blood in the water sources
2. frogs invading the land
3. the conversion of dust to lice
4. swarms of flies
5. the death of cattle and other domesticated animals
6. boils infecting man and beast
7. hail mingled with fire
8. locusts
9. darkness for three days

10. Passover.

The first nine plagues were unsuccessful however, the 10th plague met with success. In the 10th plague the god of the Jews is said to have killed the first born child and animal in every Egyptian home and barn. This same plague however passed over the homes of the "Jews" living within Egypt and as a result of this plague the "Jews" were freed.

Before the tenth plague, each Jewish family was instructed to slaughter an unblemished lamb and use it's blood to mark the door of their residence. The blood of a lamb, sheep or goat was used as an amulet, to protect the "Jews" from the tenth plague. These lambs were supposed to be one year old and they were selected on the tenth day of the newly established first month Nisan. The lambs' age symbolically represents the Earth's orbit of the Sun or the calendar year.

As dramatic as these plagues might seem they are symbolic and they represent the 11.25 days beyond the twelve natural months that are required before the year passes. Within the Jewish calendar system an 11.25 day period is accumulated for two consecutive years and midterm in the third year that 11.25 date is pro rated to help produce a supplemental 29 day month called Veadar or Adar Shemi.

Theologically and psychologically "Jesus the Christ" was assigned the name Paschal Lamb and was made one with those sacrificial lambs described in the Passover story. He was given the gentle, innocence and defenseless characteristics of lambs. "Jesus the Christ" is given credit for sacrificing his life to save the Soul of humanity in the same manner that it is claimed that lambs in the Passover story were sacrificed to save the Jews first born in Egypt. Therefore "Jesus the Christ" was supposedly crucified in the same manner that the Passover lamb was sacrificed, thereby completing their connection and oneness, while evoking sympathy, compassion and credibility for both stories.

Easter is a fabricated holiday, it is post dated, calculated and connected with Passover, so that it stays in close approximation with the fabricated "Jewish" holiday which itself, is just another perverted and contrived celebration of the vernal equinox.

The reason why the date for Easter must be calculated annually is to keep it properly associated with Passover, because the "Jewish" holiday of Passover is incorporated within the Jewish calendar, a lunar based calendar. It is based on a 354 day year while Easter is encompassed within the Gregorian calendar a solar based calendar which is based on a 365.25 day year. The Gregorian calendar is based on a fixed year while the "Jewish" calendar is based on a floating year. When these calendars are superimposed upon each other there is a tendency for days within the "Jewish" calendar, Passover included, to migrate based on the Earth year.

This migration would consistently cause Easter to come before Passover if the date set for Easter was stagnated. Ideally, Easter should always come after Passover since "Jesus the Christ" was supposedly celebrating Passover before he was killed. Therefore the formula used to calculate the dates for Easter will generally force Easter to come after Passover. However, because this formula is broad based and is designed to calculate the dates for Easter for more than two hundred years in advance, it is not accurate enough to consistently force Passover to come before Easter.

Within a two and a half to three year period, an extra month is added to the Jewish calendar to put it closer in alignment with the Earth year. This adjustment ensures that no date within the Jewish calendar migrates more than 30 days before it is brought closer into alignment with the Earth year.

The full Moon also plays an important part in the Passover story. Jewish months are based completely on lunar months, according to the book of Exodus in biblical literature. Passover occurs on the 15th day of the month, the 15th day of any natural month is a full Moon. Subsequently, Easter must come on this day since the incarnated Logos was said to be celebrating Passover before he was arrested and crucified. Or Easter must start on the next Moon phase after a full Moon since the beginning day of each Moon phase was a mini celebration of the Sun and now it is designated as Sunday and is the start of a new week.

According to biblical literature the Jewish Calendar establishes two points for the start of the year. In the first version the New Year starts in the spring while in the second version the New Year starts in the fall. The spring version is associated with Passover and the fall version is associated with autumnal equinox. The spring version occurs on the seventh month of the Jewish calendar "Nisan", it was created to validate the perverted Passover story. The Fall version occurs on the first month of the Jewish Calendar "Tishri". This version has a historical base outside of the Jewish stories and myths, because it was formulated to compliment the zodiac calendar. The fall version is officially observed by those who practice the Jewish Religion.

The ultimate manifestation of Easter and Passover can be divulged and understood by incorporating the lunar and zodiac calendar into one system. Independently, both calendars provided a dramatic advancement in civilization. However, they both encompass some inherent problems which are evident even in today's calendar. Neither calendar is completely automatic nor maintenance free. To maintain the accuracy of these calendars, periodic adjustments are required. The nature of the Earth's orbit of the Sun and the Moon's orbit of the Earth is such that it produces a natural year that is not divisible by the natural months without producing remaining days. All astronomical based calendars must deal with some form of remaining days.

Ultimately, the second level that explained Easter and Passover beyond their perverted biblical account is based on astrology and the procession of the Zodiac during the vernal equinox. The practical or critical aspect of the vernal equinox was that it was the check point to correct the lunar based calendar. From this perspective it did not matter whether the Ancient Egyptians based their month on a 30 day period as incorrectly stated by Western academia or if they based their month on a 29.5 day period as I have put forth in this book. In either case, days were left over from the 12 months year every year. If not corrected, these days would fall and accumulate into the current month or Moon count until the zodiac constellation would completely disjoint itself from it's original sign and retrogress into the previous sign.

To prevent this from occurring, a filler month was inserted after a few years to maintain the original correlation between the constellation and their respective month and zodiac. The filler month was not counted as a separate month, instead it became a part of the zodiac constellation that was currently in session. These adjustments were made during or after the vernal equinox (Easter and Passover). In this process the Moon also played another critical role. The addition of the filler month or Moon always occurred on a Moon phase to account for a more accurate calculation of time.

Moon counting was an important aspect of calendar maintenance. The Moon count started with the Moon phase which was in session during New Year's Day, the day of the Winter Solstice. This Moon phase represented the first quarter or week of the month throughout the rest of the year. Regardless of how far the New Year started within the lunar cycle there was an irrevocable link between the zodiacal constellation and the relative Moon count. The first Moon of the new year was associated with the constellation now called Aquarius, the second Moon of the new year was connected with the constellation today called Pisces. The third Moon of the new year was associated with the constellation now called Aries, the forth Moon of the new year was attached to the constellation presently called Taurus and so forth.

The time interval between the rising and setting of the Moon provides a broad window of opportunities to calculate the time of a week, month and year based on the Lunar phase and the number of Lunar cycles within a year. The Moon can be seen either day or night or both, based on the time it rises and sets, whereas, the opportunities to determine the time of year based on the Zodiac constellation are very limited. One must first posses a vivid imagination to connect a group of astronomical bodies that graphically make up a logical or tangible figure. One must be up before dawn to fix the location of the Zodiac constellations and then one must wait until the Sun rises to establish the constellation that is associated with the Sun.

The vernal equinox occurs annually when the Sun crosses the equator making night and day of equal length in all parts of the Earth. This period also signals the arrival of spring. In Ancient Egypt the arrival of spring was calculated and revered, with spring came the inundation of the Nile River and the rebirth or resurrection of vegetation; new life was brought to the normally arid and dead Sahara desert. This vegetation provided a storehouse of food for human and animal consumption. In other words Easter, even in the Christian connotation is equivalent to the celebration of spring when things that once appeared to be dead, seem to come back to life. It has nothing to do with the so called resurrection of a Jesus the Christ who in itself is a incarnated name and a metaphor for the annual arrival of spring.

The concepts of Easter, Christmas and New Years hail from the annals of Ancient Egypt. The Ancient Egyptians also created the concept now known as little Christmas during the reign of Ptolemy V Epiphany Eucharistos in 196 B.C.E. Obviously, this twelve day celebration existed long before Christianity supposedly existed and thousands of years before it was actually created.

We must remember that the Ancient Egyptians were students of nature and the cosmos. It takes the Earth 365.25 days to complete its annual orbit around the Sun, within that time span the Moon orbits the Earth 12 times, which equals 12 natural months. A lunar cycle is equal to a natural month which is equal to the time that it takes the Moon to revolve around the Earth, a lunar year equals 354 days falling appropriately 11.25 days short of a Earth year. So during the end of each year the Ancient Egyptians adjusted their lunar based year by celebrating the coming of the New Year for the additional 11.25 days that it takes to bring the lunar year in alignment with the Earth year.

This principle is known as Epact and it has been hidden to misdirect the general public from any real understanding of the Ancient Egyptian natural month calendar system. As strange as this concept might seem this same type of adjustment is taking place today. The method is different, but the objective and results are the same, to come up with a lunar year based on 12 months and 365.25 days. With the current calendar systems an adjustment is made each month, which unlike the true Ancient Egyptian system where this adjustment was made at the end of the year. Inherent within the current calendar systems, none of the months are in harmony with the lunar cycle, subsequently negating many of the natural beneficial characteristics associated with the system that the Ancient Egyptians formulated.

One and a half days are taken away from the second month, a half a day is added to the fourth, sixth, ninth and the eleventh month; while one and a half days are added to the first, third, fifth, seventh, eighth, tenth and twelfth months totaling the additional eleven days it takes to bring the lunar year in line with the Earth year. Consequently, the start of the New Year and the new month was based on the age of the current lunar cycle or the current lunar phase. If the first month during the New Year started with a half Moon, then, the following months would start with a half Moon. If the first month starts with a full Moon, then the succeeding months during the current year would start with a full Moon.

The term Epact is an esoteric concept which denotes all of the implications and ramifications which was the result of harmonizing the lunar year with the Earth year, as previously discussed. Each year, the New Year would start approximately six hours later, thereby, gradually advancing the calendar by one day every four years.

Millenniums later, the Ancient Egyptians overrode those eleven days that were traditionally set aside to celebrate the New Year , so that they could honor and give thanks to Ptolemy V, Epiphany Eucharistos for forgiving past debt and taxes that he had imposed and were owed by the Coptic priest society.

James Henry Breasted, considered the father of Egyptology, in 1919, with the financial backing of John D. Rockefeller, founded the Oriental Institute at the University of Chicago. The Oriental Institute is considered the foremost institution concerning Ancient Egypt and related subjects. Egyptology is a discipline that was created by Breasted and his contemporaries to politically control the interpretation and dissemination of the research coming out of Egypt related to Ancient Egypt.

Breasted and his companions conveniently designated the genesis for the Ancient Egyptians year as the day of the Vernal Equinox, this diversion along with others, has two functions (1) to effectively throw the world off the true path concerning the Ancient Egyptians and the subsequent development of civilization, the origin of man made religions and the influence of Western societies. (2) to give the incarnated "Jews" or "Hebrews" a more conceptual foundation by creating for them a separate time concept which in part is based on the Ancient Egyptians real time concept of natural or lunar months. The chronology of Egypt is another misconception introduced by Breasted and his colleague E. Meyers. It is an artificial format and timetable superimposed on the history of Ancient Egypt based on biblical literature. It is used to trivialize the Ancient Egyptian scientific, engineering, mathematical and cultural achievements while it falsely inserts a violent, ruthless and greedy past.

Christianity is the driver of "Western Civilization". Christianity secretly represents the Earth's orbit of the Sun while "Jesus the Christ" is the corrupt vicar of the Sun. Ultimately Christianity and the other major World religions are allegories pertaining to the importance of the Sun. All four GEO/SOLAR OCCURRENCES are shadowed or paralleled by superficial Western holidays. These superficial holidays esoterically denote the true significance of the four GEO/SOLAR OCCURRENCES. The Summer Solstice is paralleled by Shavout and Father's Day. The Autumnal Equinox is shadowed by Rosh Hashana. Christmas, New Year's Day and Hanukkah together are the corrupted mimesis for the Winter Solstice. Saint Patrick's Day (March 17), Easter and Passover are the perverted mimesis for the Vernal Equinox. (p.44)

Land markers or monuments were created and can be positioned to align with the Sun rising and the Sun setting to indicate the time and arrival of the Winter Solstice, the Vernal Equinox, the Summer Solstice, and the Autumnal Equinox.

In the Northern hemisphere the winter solstice under the current calendar format, takes place around December 21st. The winter solstice occurs at the time of the year or at that point in the Earth's orbit where the Sun appears to have no further southward motion or when it reaches its most southern point. This point signals the actual start of winter. It is the day with the least amount of Sunlight, New Year's Day, defined as the first day of the calendar. But the first day of the year depends upon the calendar being used within a cyclical system. Any point can be designated as the starting point. According to the Gregorian calendar which was introduced in the 1500's, January 1 is recognized as New Year's Day.

The weekday assigned as New Year's Day varies from year to year. The 365.25 day year contains 52 (7 day) weeks plus 1.25 days. This forces New Year's Day to come on consecutive weekdays for three years and during the fourth year (leap year) New Year's Day advances two weekdays; however, for Ancient Egyptians who were directly in line with nature this day would coincide with a natural Solar occurrence, the Vernal/Autumnal Equinox or the Summer/Winter Solstice.

The Gregorian calendar was contrived during the Renaissance Era, an era that was notorious for the divestment of the Ancient and Coptic Egyptians as the source of the world's knowledge base. The Renaissance is equally known for the dissemination of the lies, deception, and duplicity which helped to define and promote Western philosophy as the source of the world's knowledge base. In the Northern hemisphere, where the Ancient Egyptians formatted and formulated a concept of time, this day was the Winter Solstice and the beginning of the new year.

We must remember that in each instance whenever the Coptic Egyptians created customs, laws or ceremonies for Christianity, it was always based on a previous Ancient Egyptian practice. In both cases, the winter solstice and the vernal equinox are natural holidays revered by the Ancient Egyptians. They are synonymous with the birth and resurrection of the Sun which was eventually perverted and translated into Christmas (Mass for Christ) and Easter.

The Horus/Osiris (Ausara) principle is the metaphor for the Earth's entire ecology system. Since Osiris (Ausara), the Ancient Egyptian God, is considered God of the Underworld, God of Vegetation and the Sun of the Sun or the Sun of the Creator, he serves as the model and forerunner of the incarnated Logos (Jesus the Christ).

There was a transitional god/created creature, who served as a critical link between Osiris (Ausara) and "Jesus the Christ" but since has been erased from the pages of history. Thanks to Dr. Walter Williams and his powerful book, The Historical Origin of Christianity, for revealing this critical key and powerful connection. The name of this creature is Serapis. Serapis was dismissed because its presence would reveal the real symbolism behind Christianity rather than the pretentious meaning that Christianity has today.

Politically, the creation of Serapis and the subsequent creation of "Christ" represented an all out attempt to get the Ancient Egyptians and their offspring to worship an European image as a god. The concept of a resurrection of a "Jesus the Christ" is only a metaphor for the arrival of spring. Astronomically, the Vernal Equinox (the resurrection of the Sun or spring) signals that point in the Earth's orbit when the Sun appears to rise or resurrect itself above the southern hemisphere and crosses the equator into the northern hemisphere. This occurrence is actually the result of the Earth oscillating as it orbits the Sun- rather than the Sun oscillating with respect to the Earth. Geologically, the Vernal Equinox represents the time of year when vegetation in the Northern hemisphere resurrects itself. For that reason, whenever you read anything pertaining to Horus/ Osiris (Ausara), the European educational community attempts to define the Horus/Osiris (Ausara) concept as a local and provincial concept. Deceptively, this is an attempt to confine and marginalize this principle to a particular area and time in Ancient Egyptians history rather than exposing the Horus/Osiris (Ausara) principle as being the powerful, far reaching, universal principle that was critical in transforming the Ancient Egyptians civilization from inception, as well as creating the foundation for the entire world's political, spiritual, scientific, and educational institutions millenniums later. "Jesus the Christ" is the perverted mimesis for Horus/Osiris (Ausara), and the Horus/Osiris (Ausara) principle is the metaphor for the birth or start of the New Year and the arrival of spring or the Vernal Equinox.

The so called Jewish calendar is merely a variation of the Moorish calendar which is predated and ascribed to a non historical people called Jews. It adopts the ancient Egyptians natural months system by alternating 29 and 30 day months. Thereby coming up with months that average 29.5 days and a base year which contains only 354 days. This artificial calendar is adjusted within a two and a half to three year period (seven times in every nineteen years), with the addition of an extra (29 days) month Veadar or Adar Sheni. Subsequently, a "Jewish" year can contain anywhere from 354 days to 383 days. The Moslem calendar is merely a variation of the so called natural month calendar.

Note : *Although the actual period for 12 natural months or the Lunar year is 354.3670 days with a remainder of 10.8921 days to complete the Earth year, the Ancient Egyptians recognized and observed the Lunar year with 354 days with 11.25 days to complete the Earth year.*

The Paradox Of The Year

It is interesting to note that Western reference sources, including Western College Dictionaries claim that the Earth's orbital cycle of the Sun yields several different intervals for the length of the year.

1). Tropical equinoctial or Earth year
The period from the vernal equinox to the vernal equinox (365 days, 5 hours, 48 minutes and 46 seconds).

2). Sidereal year (365 days 6 hours, 9 minutes and 9.54 seconds).
The period it takes the Sun to pass from a fixed star and back to the same position.

3). Anomalistic year (from perihelion to perihelion) or, December Solstice to December Solstice. (365 days, 6 hours, 13 minutes and 53 seconds).

I question and challenge the validity of such a declaration because it is contradictory, confusing and illogical.

This paradox is extended when it is revealed that Western society designates January 1, as the start of the New Year, while it applies the time interval associated with the vernal equinox, even though the December Solstice time interval starts within two weeks from this date.

This contradiction became even more problematic when we examined the consequences of having more than one time interval based on the same cycle, when extending the time frame beyond a year as required when dealing with calendar maintenance.

This discrepancy becomes even more obvious when we use the time interval associated with the vernal equinox, and if we add an extra day every four years to compensate for the 5 hours, 48 minutes and 44 seconds that is not added during the calendar year. The sum of these four partial days is 23 hours 15 minutes and 4 seconds, an adjustment is required because the leap year day added is overstated by 44 minutes and 56 seconds. The Gregorian calendar addresses this problem by adding a day to the calendar every four years except in years that are not divisible by 400 without leaving a remainder.

If the tropical equinoctial year is used, in addition to the leap year day every four years, an extra day must be added to the calendar every 128.1899 years to compensate for the understatement of the leap year day by 44 minutes and 56 seconds (23 hours and 15 minutes and 4 seconds).

If the anomalistic year is used, in addition to the leap year day every four years, an extra day must be subtracted from the calendar every 103.7214 days to compensate for the overstatement of the leap year day by 55 minutes and 32 seconds (24 hours and 55 minutes and 32 seconds).

At this point it becomes obvious that there is something inherently wrong with claiming more than one interval for the same cycle. If this annual cycle actually yields more than one interval, an extra day must be added to the calendar every 128.1899 years and a day must be subtracted from the calendar every 103.7214 days. These two operations would virtually counteract each other and since Western societies use the Gregorian calendar we can be sure that both arithmetic operations are not preformed.

Father's Day, and the Earth's Orbit of the Sun

Every year Father's day is celebrated either on the Sunday of, or on the Sunday before, the first day of Summer. This date is strategically placed on the third Sunday of June, thus making sure that Father's day and the Summer Solstice like St. Patrick's Day and the Vernal Equinox holidays always occur within a week of each other. This holiday supposedly is a celebration and recognition of fatherhood in the United States. However, upon closer examination Father's Day can be divulged as an indirect celebration for the day of the Summer Solstice, since Western culture does not celebrate the June Solstice directly.

The Ancient Egyptians having the first and oldest civilization on Earth, recognize Osiris (Ausara) as the first father on Earth. Every year the Summer Solstice occurs either on the 21st or 22nd of June. It must be stated that all Western and Ancient Calendars are derived from the Ancient Egyptians, these calendars and their secret counterparts, Western and Eastern religions, tell the story of Earth's annual journey around the Sun. The architects of the United States government were members of the Masonic order. Note that: Masonic organizations are transitional societies that serve as a link between the wisdom of the Ancient Egyptians and the corrupt modern world. The foundation of masonry is found in the knowledge and symbols of the Ancient Egyptians, however perverted. Ancient Egyptian principles and Western religious theologies and philosophies are also incorporated into masonry, thereby given its mission of establishing Western institutions; therefore, the so called founding fathers incorporated elements of Ancient Egyptians civilization into the United States and other Western societies.

In the Ancient Egyptians creation story, the Ennead, Horus and Osiris (Ausara) are conceptual entities identified with the Sun, Horus is identified with the Winter Solstice and within this book, for the first time I am associating Osiris (Ausara) with the Summer Solstice, in terms of the period of Sunlight within a day. In the Northern Hemisphere the Sun and the day are at their most infantile state during the Winter Solstice. This is when the Sun rises lower in the southeast, stays low, and sets lowest in the southwest, the shortest day of the year. In contrast the Sun and the day are at their most mature and dominant state during the Summer Solstice. This is the day when the Sun rises in the northeast, climbs high in the sky and sets in the northwest. The longest day of the year.

Consequently, Horus is symbolic of the birth of the Sun and is characterized as an infant, conversely, Osiris (Ausara) is identified as an adult male, and is characterized by the relative strength and length of Sunlight that this day brings, and is deemed the Father. The Ancient Egyptians family based divine triad consists of a Father, Mother and child. Osiris (Ausara the father, Amon-Ra the Creator), the Son of the Sun (Horus) and Isis (Aset) the Holy Cow or Holy Mother). Christian theology at its most fundamental level emulates the Ancient Egyptians Creation story with the exception that the Christian Trinity encompasses an unnatural family as its triad, comprising male members only (the Father

,the Son and the Holy Ghost). In Christian theology "Jesus the Christ" is made one with the Father (God). In addition Christian theology recognizes the person who occupies the Office of Pope as the Vicar and representative of "Jesus the Christ". The term Pope literally means father.

In the Northern Hemisphere the Sun appears to be at its most dominant position during the June or Summer Solstice. Father's day was created to mark the Summer Solstice without alerting the general population to its importance or relevance, thereby preventing the masses from making a direct correlation between religious theology and the Summer Solstice or any of the other GEO/SOLAR OCCURRENCES. If this critical link became obvious it would help deplete Western religions of their mysticism and authority. For Western religions would be exposed at their most fundamental level, the hidden representative of the calendar year. The Summer Solstice is the meridian and climax of the year, it is the natural indicator of Earth's half way journey around the Sun.

The Seasons and the Earth's Orbit of the Sun

Since explaining how the Western world propagates as facts, the change in seasons, which I dismissed as a theory in Book I, I would like to present my findings for this dismissal, but, before proceeding I would like to reiterate some general facts about this subject.

There are five climatic regions of Earth. The frigid zones, lying within the Arctic and Antarctic circles. The temperate zones bounded by the frigid zones and the Tropics and the Torrid zone including the Tropic of Cancer and the Tropic of Capricorn. The frigid zones are regions that never experience hot weather, for most of the year these regions are very cold and frozen. The Torrid zone climate is always warm, hot and Sunny, the weather within the temperate zone varies greatly; it ranges from cold weather in the winter to warm and hot weather in the summer.

The Winter and Summer Solstices, and the Vernal and Autumnal Equinoxes are natural phenomenons which occur annually and they mark the beginning of the four seasons.

When it is winter in the Northern Hemisphere, it is summer in the Southern Hemisphere, when it is spring in the Northern Hemisphere , it is fall in the Southern Hemisphere. When it is summer in the Northern Hemisphere, it is winter in the Southern Hemisphere, and when it is fall in the Northern Hemisphere, it is spring in the Southern Hemisphere. Hence, the progression of seasons in the Northern Hemisphere winter, spring, summer and fall correlate with the Winter Solstice, the Vernal Equinox, the Summer Solstice and the Autumnal Equinox. While in the Southern Hemisphere the correlations are the Summer Solstice, Autumnal Equinox, Winter Solstice and Vernal Equinox.

In the tropic zones there are only small fluctuations in temperature during the year. However, there are prolonged periods of rainfall and long periods without much rain. This yearly cycle alternates between the Tropic of Cancer and Tropic of Capricorn and is known respectively as wet season and dry season.

Daylight savings time was developed as a result of the seasonal changes in Sunlight. Daylight savings time is concerned with making an adjustment to standard time to take advantage of the increasing amount of Sunlight available during the Spring and Summer months. In the United States daylight savings time starts the first Sunday in April and ends the last Sunday of October. Daylight savings time occurs when standard time is advanced an hour; it is used to give an hour more of daylight at the end of the usual working day. At the end of this period the time is set back an hour to re-establish standard time. Daylight savings time was first used in England during World War I. Today many countries around the world have adopted this principle.

The extremities of Sunlight vary so greatly, that in the polar regions the year is divided into two seasons, a light and dark season. The outer limits of the Arctic circle lie 66 degrees and 30 minutes north latitude and the outer limits of the Antarctic circle lie 66 degrees and 30 minutes south latitude. The Arctic and Antarctic circle are imaginary rings that have the North pole and South pole as their center. The Arctic circle consists of the ice cover Arctic Ocean with the northern sections of Scandinavia, Russia, Canada and Alaska at it's outer limits. The Antarctic circle consists of the Antarctica continent which is extended further by polar ice pack surrounded by the Antarctic ocean. The Midnight Sun is a principle that describes 24 hours of uninterrupted Sunlight. This condition occurs in the Arctic and Antarctic circles. In the Arctic circle this state occurs for a few days around June 22. It also occurs at the Antarctic circle during the winter solstice for a similar period. At the North pole the Sun never sets for six months, from March 20 through September 23. In the South Pole, The Sun never rises for that same period of time. At the South

Pole the Sun remains above the horizon from September 23 through March 20. During this same interval the Sun never rises at the North pole; therefore, the North and South Poles alternate, between six months of uninterrupted Sunlight and six months without direct Sunlight, a state which ranges from a dusk or dawn like state to total darkness. The length of intervals of continuous Sunlight decreases as the distance from either pole increases.

The Obelisk as a component of a Sundial

The upper and lower processions of the Earth's orbit produce a region on Earth where there is little or no change in the weather and the amount of Sunlight year round. This region is called the tropic zone. At the center of the tropic zone is the equator. The Northern portion of the tropic zone is called the Tropic of Cancer and the Southern portion of this zone is called the Tropic of Capricorn. The Sunlight for the outer extremity of the tropic zone ranges from 10½ to 13½ hours per day, depending on the season. The tropic zone extends 1600 miles north and south of the equator.

It has been speculated that the Ancient Egyptians possibly used the obelisk as a component of a Sundial to tell time, the Sundial being a circular device with markings around its outer edge and with an angular or rod shape object standing erected at its center. This angular object casts a shadow over the various Sundial markings as the Sun appears to track across the sky thereby, indicating the time based upon the Sun's movement. However, the equator is the only region on Earth where a Sundial can be used with any type of accuracy because it is the only region that receives the same amount of Sunlight year round. In other regions during the year, the amount of Sunlight varies from day to day. Given, the largest portion of the region that is traditionally denoted as Egypt exists hundreds of miles north of the Tropic of Cancer, it is highly unlikely that the Ancient Egyptians used this concept to tell time. Unless of course an adjustment was factored into the time, based on the Moon count or zodiac, to compensate for the daily difference in Sunlight. Otherwise the discrepancy would be greater than the hour and half inconsistency which occurs in the tropic zone.

Oriental Africa and the Sun

In Oriental Africa or the Nile Valley the observation of the Sun was a critical task. The term Orient or Oriental goes far beyond it's superficial connotation of a racial type of people living in Asia. Today known as Chinese, Japanese and Korean, etc. The term Orient ultimately means to adjust or adapt to the Sun. This term applies to migratory animals who, each year, follow the Sun south and later back north in quest for a more habitable environment. Historically, and culturally it refers directly to the Ancient Egyptians who initiated the concept and made the Sun the central theme in their civilization. This concept was later adopted by subsequent cultures. The change in seasons and Sunlight comes as a result of the Earth's daily longitudinal and latitudinal change in its orbit of the Sun. Because of these modifications, the Sun appears to take a different path across the sky every day.

Originally, the whole African continent was Oriental, but, with the start of Hellenization, a process that began after the Greeks invaded Egypt, the people of the Nile Valley began to migrate further into the interior of Africa (the Sudan and Ethiopia). The influence of the Sun was gradually diminished. Cultures living outside of the tropic zone were more likely to be governed by the dictates of the Sun's movements (as opposed to Africans who lived within the tropic region). Because the tropic is conducive to a more stable environment year round.

The tropic zone maintains approximately twelve hours of Sunlight year round; therefore, the tropic regions do not go through diverse periods or seasons. The environment year round is conducive to plant cultivation and plant regeneration. This ensures an abundance of food year round. For people living outside of the tropic zone the seasons determine the weather environment, when to plant crops and when to harvest crops. The season also determines the availability of and hunting seasons for, certain animals. Every element that man needs to survive comes either directly from plant life or indirectly from animal. Clothing is an important factor, food is even more of an important consideration. In the autumn and winter months, plant life outside of the tropic becomes barren or dies. If a community did not prepare for this situation by storing food and the making of clothing, they would either starve to death or freeze to death during this period. In addition, if these conditions could not be predicted and accounted for, then civilization could not and would not have advanced because there would have been a preoccupation with wandering and not knowing what the future would bring.

During the year, under the cover of clouds, the shifting levels of Sunlight which occurs during the Solar day, the period between Sunrise and Sunset, often goes unnoticed. Perhaps it is this reason why the Ancient Egyptians chose the Sahara desert and the Nile Valley to anchor their civilization. In the desert the skies almost always remain clear. Therefore, by day and by night the atmosphere could be studied without much obstruction from clouds. Generally, the weather for any given season or any given region is determined by the location of the Earth in its orbit of the Sun. However, the atmosphere or prevailing winds plays an unpredictable secondary role in this formula. For example in the heart of winter in Chicago the weather has changed to a temperature that one would expect in late spring. In these cases the prevailing winds have their origins in the southern regions where the weather is warmer because of the additional Sunlight it receives during this time of year.

The silhouette of the Earth's orbit is said to be elliptical, which means that the distance between the Earth and Sun is not constant, but varies from day to day. The innermost point of this orbit is called the perihelion, at this point the Sun is said to be 91,400,000 miles away from Earth. The outer most distance is called the aphelion and at this point the Sun is said to be 94,500,000 miles away from Earth. What is fascinating about this concept is that neither the perihelion or the aphelion has a net effect on the Earth as far as regulating temperatures or governing the change of seasons on Earth . Even though the differences between these two points is thought to be three million miles. Nonetheless, at any given point within the Earth's annual orbit of the Sun, the Northern Hemisphere and the Southern Hemisphere are experiencing opposite seasons.

The Wave Theory and The Earth's Orbit of the Sun

As stated earlier in Book I, Western academia in its attempt to control world academia offers an erroneous and oversimplified explanation of how and why the seasons change. This theory is based on the notion that the Earth revolves around the Sun tilted on a 23.5 degree angle, and as the Earth orbits the Sun, the Northern and Southern Hemisphere are exposed to inverse amounts of Sunlight based on the Earth's position in its orbit. Thus causing a change in season at certain fixed points.

However, when you research this topic you will most likely find a diagram, featuring a pair of graphics of the Earth 180 degrees apart or opposite, with the Sun at the center. This diagram represents the Earth as it moves around the Sun. Each graphic of the Earth represents the Earth experiencing a Solstice, the December Solstice and the June Solstice. Based on this graphic, this 23.5 degree tilt, positions the Northern Hemisphere in a direct line of the Sun's light, at one end of the view, causing summer in the Northern Hemisphere and winter in the Southern Hemisphere and at the opposite end it positions the Southern Hemisphere in a direct line of light producing summer in the Southern Hemisphere and winter in the Northern Hemisphere. This diagram may be convincing at some level, but there are two major issues that should be resolved but cannot be resolved. First there are four GEO/SOLAR OCCURRENCES in a year not just two. The Vernal Equinox and the Autumnal Equinox are not demonstrated or shown. And the reason for their absence, is that it is impossible to depict the Equinoxes based on this theory and in this graphic. Because the Equinox represents a period in time when every place on Earth experiences an equal amount of Sunlight at the same time, at no point in the Earth's orbit is the 23.5 degree tilt not in play, therefore if the diagram of the two solstices and the Sun are correct, this makes it impossible to demonstrate a consistent follow-through for the Equinoxes because the Earth is tilted. It is also impossible to demonstrate a consistent follow through for the gradual shifting of light between the Northern Hemisphere and Southern Hemisphere, therefore this theory is erroneous.

However, this theory leaves many unanswered questions, so I have submitted the following theory. The dynamics which occur between the Sun and the Earth that causes the changes in the seasons, are as follows:

As the Earth revolves around the Sun, it does not stay on one plane. The Earth, acts as if it is set in a gigantic wave, its latitude based on the Sun equator's gradual rises and falls as it completes its annual cycle. The frequency of this wave results in one cycle or orbit per year.

This wave promotes a gradual change in the amount and angle of Sunlight that the Earth receives in any region as well as the changing temperatures and seasons which accompany the Earth in these regions throughout it's annual cycle.

The Sun, like the Earth, is a sphere shaped object. The nature of any sphere shape is to protrude where it obtains its center of mass. The circumference of any sphere object is greatest at its center. Therefore, subsequently, whatever portion of the Earth's surface that is closest to or in line with the Sun's equator receives the greatest concentration of the Sun's energy.

As the Earth moves up and down this wave, the Northern and Southern Hemispheres are inversely exposed to varying amounts of Sunlight, depending upon whether the Earth's equator is above, below or equal to the Sun's equator. Because the greatest intensity of the Sun's energies is delivered at the Sun's equator, as the Earth rides its wave, the angle and exposure of light to the Earth's surface changes, thereby, causing a change in seasons. At any given time the hemisphere which is closest to the Sun's equator is experiencing summer. Inversely the hemisphere which is furthest from the Sun's equator is experiencing winter.

The Earth's poles do not stay at a constant angle throughout it's orbit. The forces exerted on the Earth by the Sun cause the Earth's poles to shift like a pendulum to and fro. During the Winter Solstice the Earth's poles are tilted to a degree which exposes the Southern Hemisphere to an excessive amount of Sunlight while shielding the Northern Hemisphere of normal Sunlight. And, during the Vernal Equinox the Earth's poles become erect or perpendicular to the Sun's equator exposing the entire Earth's surface to even Sunlight and during the Summer Solstice the angle of the Earth has changed to expose the Northern Hemisphere to excessive amounts of Sunlight while denying normal Sunlight to the Southern Hemisphere. During the Autumnal Equinox once again the Earth's poles are perpendicular to the Sun's equator allowing for an even distribution of Sunlight to the Earth's surface. (p.44)

After the day of the winter solstice, the Earth starts to ascend toward the Sun's equator. This results in an increase in the duration of the solar days in the Northern Hemisphere and a decrease in the duration of the solar days in the Southern Hemisphere. When the Earth's equator becomes parallel with the Sun's equator , this phenomenon is known as the Vernal/Autumnal Equinox. It is the period when there are 12 hours of Sunlight and darkness in both the Northern and Southern Hemispheres. As the Earth continues its descension, the days in the Northern Hemisphere get longer as the days in the Southern Hemisphere get shorter. When the Earth approaches the lowest point in its orbit and wave, the Earth starts its ascent and the reverse occurs, the Summer Solstice.

As demonstrated by the gradual changes in temperature during the

Earth's orbit of the Sun, the days of the Winter Solstice, Vernal Equinox, Summer Solstice and the Autumnal Equinox, represent the midpoint of the days typified by their respective seasons, short days, average days, long days and average days rather than the starting point of these seasons. That is the twenty one longest days of the year do not occur after the Summer Solstice, but rather ten days before and ten days after the Summer Solstice. In a similar mode the twenty shortest days of the year do not occur after the Winter Solstice, but ten days before and ten days after the Winter Solstice.

Two of the most awesome phenomenons which occur in nature are the mechanics that cause plants to go into a suspended state of animation during fall and then come out of this condition during spring. These occurrences have less to do with the amount of moisture and warmth that plants experience during spring and fall, and more to do with the total amount of Sunlight that plants receive. Of all the processes that contribute to plant life, Sunlight is paramount.

Photosynthesis, is the process in which green plants convert light energy into chemical energy, thereby causing several chain reactions; this ultimately results in plant growth and the release of oxygen as a by-product. Even on cloudy days, most of the Sun's light reaches the ground. Both the Vernal and Autumnal Equinoxes are transitional periods which occur concurrently each year. This period is unique and is characterized by having an equal amount of Sunlight and darkness within a 24 hour day. The occurrences which cause plants to hibernate or come out of this suspended state is triggered by an area getting more or less than twelve hours of Sunlight per day. The amount of rainfall and the average temperature of a region vary from year to year. The only factor that does not vary is the amount of Sunlight these plants receive on any given day, a factor which is predetermined every day within a year by the Earth's orbit of the Sun.

It takes the Earth 186 days to travel from the Vernal Equinox to the Autumnal Equinox . However, it only takes the Earth 179 days to travel from the Autumnal Equinox to the Vernal Equinox. This process can be further refined by measuring the number of days between each solar occurrence. When this is done one can see that these periods follow a definite pattern. The period from the Winter Solstice to the Vernal Equinox requires 90 days, the span from the Vernal Equinox to the Summer Solstice requires 92 days. The interval from the Summer

Solstice to the Autumnal Equinox demands 94 days and the time between the Autumnal Equinox to the Winter Solstice takes 89 days. Now one can deduce that the shortest distance between the Sun and the Earth is the day of the winter solstice. By using the equinoxes as midpoint one can see that the two shortest periods of the GEO/SOLAR OCCURRENCES are leading up to and moving away from the Winter Solstice.

Spring signifies that time of year when each day for the next six months or 186 days will receive more than twelve hours of Sunlight. Fall, the hyphenation period is designated when the amount of Sunlight falls below twelve hours for the next 179 days. In the Northern Hemisphere the period between the Autumnal and the Vernal Equinoxes is like turning on an oven for thirty minutes verses the period between the Vernal Equinox to the Autumnal Equinox which is like turning on a refrigerator for thirty five minutes. There is a significant increase in the amount of Sunlight and heat during this interval.

The Sun and the significance of the number Twelve

Finally, the number twelve has an important place throughout human history as well as most, if not all, man made religions. The significance of the number twelve can be extracted from the twelve lunar months plus the 11.5 days (12 days) that it takes the Earth to revolve around the Sun. Concepts such as the twelve tribes of Israel, the twelve knights of the round table, the twelve days of Christmas, the twelve person jury in a U.S. trial, the twelve zodiac signs, the twelve chromatic tones and scales in modern music and the twelve hours on a clock are symbolic of the twelve lunar months. The Chinese calendar is based on a twelve year cycle which features one of twelve different animals each year. Every year is expressed by its numeric value alone with the designation that it is the year of the Rat, Ox, Tiger, Hare, Dragon, Snake, Horse, Goat, Monkey, Rooster, Dog or Pig. What is interesting about this twelve year cycle is that like the twelve month cycle it denotes an important natural cycle which is the biological cycle from birth to young adulthood. Since children start puberty primarily between the ages of twelve and thirteen years, this cycle was used to denote when a child or a group of children will become adolescents. This period in many ancient societies represented both a change in status and eligibility to individuals or to groups who obtained this status. With this new status came additional rights and privileges. The orbit of Jupiter around the Sun and the Solar cycle also occurs within a twelve Earth year period.

However, the most powerful illustration and depiction of the linkage that exists between the solar principles and the solar and lunar calendars and Western religions is the myth of "Jesus the Christ" and the Last Supper. "The Christ birth" takes place in the twelfth month. At the age of twelve "Jesus the Christ" is said to come into worldly knowledge at a level that astonished those who heard him. The Last Supper depicts thirteen Caucasian men seated at a banquet table. The incarnated central character "Jesus the Christ" is seated in the seventh position. Behind the head of "Christ" is a halo, this disk actually represents the Sun. In Christian theology "Christ" is said to be the Son, but the actual translation is the Sun.

According to the biblical story, the Last Supper literature represents the last meal that "Jesus the Christ" had before he was betrayed by one of his disciples and later crucified by the Romans. However, Dr. Walter Williams in his powerful book "The Historical Origin of Christianity" reveals that the concept of the Last Supper was originally a ritualistic honor associated with what is now called the Eucharist. The Eucharist means Thanksgiving. The Greeks and the Romans toasted and saluted the image of Serapis during the last meal of the day. Ultimately, the substance behind the symbolic Last Supper is that "Jesus the Christ" represents the Sun or (Ra) and each of the 12 apostles or disciples represent the twelve natural months or Moons that it takes the Earth to complete it's orbit around the Sun.

The number twelve was so important in the Ancient Egyptian culture, when one analyzes the Ennead beyond the obvious, one will find that there are actually twelve Deities or twelve destined characters inclusive within the Ennead rather than the nine that are initially highlighted. The additional deities who are not mentioned, but who are synonymous with Horus and Nut respectively are Osiris (Ausara), Ihy and Hathor. The number twelve was ultimately symbolized in Ancient Egypt on the gold-plated backrest of "Tutankhamun's" throne, where Ra (the Sun) is depicted with twelve rays or arms.

Natural cycles and the significance of the numbers four, seven, nine, thirteen, nineteen and twenty four

Numerology is a theological principle which not only pervaded religious systems but secular matters as well. Supposedly it is a system that combines logic with numbers; however, if these numbers do not have a basis in nature and if these numbers do not involve natural cycles, then they are just another superficial myth.

The number three is the first of a serial of prime numbers that symbolically represent powerful concepts in nature, which will be discussed in the next section.

The number four supersedes all the other numbers in symbolic importance, except the number three, because it represents the government of the Earth's environment and life cycle, Winter Solstice, Vernal Equinox, Summer Solstice and Autumnal Equinox. Today the business world pays homage to the number four by dividing the business year into quarters.

The importance of the number seven is derived from the lunar phases which change on average every 7.3826 days. It takes the Moon an average of 7.3826 days to go from one phase to another phase. This period constitutes a natural week and is the foundation of the modern week and the number seven.

The number nine symbolically represents human birth by representing the nine months of human gestation. The Ancient Egyptians mimic this concept and cleverly applied the symbolism of the number nine to their creation story the Ennead. They symbolically encoded the importance of the nine months of human gestation by translating the nine months of procreation to the nine deities who bring forth creation. Additionally, astronomically the number nine represents the nine known planets which orbit the Sun. The Ennead literally means nine deities.

Although the number twelve represents, the number of complete natural months and additional days that it takes the Earth to complete its orbit of the Sun. The number thirteen also receives a great amount of prominence as the total number of whole plus partial natural months that it takes to complete an Earth year.

The importance of the number nineteen goes beyond the limits of a year. The metonic cycle is based on a nineteen year cycle. This period constitutes 235 lunations. Historically, it was deceptively disassociated from the Ancient Egyptian calendar system and falsely ascribed to the Roman calendar. The number nineteen is important to any calendar system based on natural months, particularly the so called "Jewish

Calendar" which represents the elapsed time the new Moon and the full Moon returns to the same day of the year. In other words after 19 years, the differences which exist between a lunar year and a Earth year are inherently corrected or rectified to the extent that the lunar year and the Earth year coincide and start over again without any remaining days left from previous years. The Ancient Egyptians expressed this concept with nineteen hands or rays extending from the Sun (Amon-Ra).

The clock is a perfect symbolic representative of the lunar based year. The term clockwise describes both the movement and direction the Earth travels in its orbit of the Sun. The hour hand on the clock mimics the Earth's movement around the Sun. The minute hand represents the Moon's movement around the Earth and the second hand symbolizes the Earth revolving on it axis. In the course of one Earth year, the lunar year and calendar goes through two twelve period cycles. The first cycle includes months and the second cycle involves days. When totaling the number 12 from the first cycle and the number 12 from the second cycle the sum is 24. By dividing the day into 24 equal parts this symbolic number is used to create the period known as the hour. To symbolically represent the lunar based year in one day, the clock and time is formatted in two 12 hour periods one is known as A.M. and the other period is known as P.M. It is no coincidence that the direction of a circle is expressed with the number 360 or 360 degrees. This number is symbolic of the 365.25 days that it takes the Earth to orbit the Sun, if this number was not symbolic it could be represented by any arbitrary number 120, 180, 500 or 720....etc.

The Ancient Egyptian Divine Triad / Divine Time Trilogy and the number three

The Ancient Egyptians used the number three to represent their divine Trinity, The Father, the Sun and the Holy Cow. The pyramid site at Giza ultimately reflects the foundation of the Ancient Egyptians time concept by mirroring the Ancient Egyptians divine triad. The Great pyramid of Giza represents the Sun, the second pyramid of Giza represents the Earth and the third pyramid of Giza represents the Moon. The Ancient Egyptians Divine Time Trilogy incorporates The Sun, Earth and the Moon, the three components that establish the original and natural time concept. According to the Ennead the Sun is the creative force and the source of the Earth and the Moon. The Earth is deemed (Mother Earth) and is the source of life. In the Ennead, Nut and Geb were born together (atmosphere and the Earth). Also Ihy, the Ancient Egyptian deity who is one with Horus, is said to be the Astronomical offspring of Ra (the Sun) and Nut (the sky), thus giving Horus his Astronomical identity as the Son of the Sun or the (Moon). From Earth the Moon mirrors the light from the Sun, providing light to the Earth after dark symbolically making the Moon a miniature Sun or the Sun (Son) of the Sun. Ihy is pronounced the same as eye that biological organ which provides humans with sight. Symbolically the eye of Horus or Ihy (the Moon) provides the Earth with physical light at night, like the Sun during the day. The four Sun's of Horus (the four Canonic Jars used in the Ancient Egyptians embalming process) represents the four phases of the Moon.

In addition the three hand's of the modern clock are systematically arranged in the order of their magnitude like the three principle pyramids of Giza, to reflect the astronomical alignment of the Sun, Earth and Moon. The hour hand represents the Sun and the year, the minute hand represents the Earth and the four seasons. The second hand represents the month and the Moon. Also, the importance of the number three can be relegated to the number of Moons or months which occur from one solar occurrence to another solar occurrence.

THE ANCIENT EGYPTIAN DIVINE TRIAD

Astronomical Body	Astronomical Name	Human Name	Human Title
The Sun	Ra	Osiris (Ausara)	The Father (the Sun)
The Moon	Ihy	Horus	The Sun (son) of the Sun
The Earth	Hathor	Isis (Aset)	The Holy Cow (mother of the Sun of the Sun)

The Earth's orbit of Sun and the development of Western Institutions

The Ancient Egyptians lived in a holistic society. Their temple system was the embodiment of what is now divided into educational, spiritual and governmental institutions. To institutionalize was to deify and make sacred. The formulation of civilization was the product of the accumulation of critical environmental and Solar knowledge. From these principles came:

1. A understanding of the Earth's orbit of the Sun and the concept of time.
2. A respect for life and nature resulting in a sense of spirituality
3. The establishment of a formalized government resulting in manifestation of high civilization.

The temple system was the reservoir and depository for learned men and women who studied and observed the consequences of the solar and lunar cycles in particular and nature in general. The first phase of temple development was educational, from this phase came a time concept. Many of the mysteries of life were unlocked by the time concept, establishing order and a map into the future.

The second phase was spiritual, from this phase came the symbols which ultimately developed into a writing system. Symbols were created to represent significant events in the year; these symbols were later formatted into stories. These stories and symbols were revered because they contained key information. The Ancient Egyptians understood that they were not completely in control of their fate, therefore they decided to honor the creative forces of the Universe in general and Solar knowledge in particular.

And, on the third and final level, the social and political plane, information was further entrenched into the Ancient Egyptian's society by forming a government that symbolically acts out those natural laws installed in their creation stories. These stories highlighted and depicted the critical solar information in the administration of their government functions on a daily basis, thus creating the foundation for governing.

The divine right of kingship in Europe is grounded in Ancient Egyptians culture. It is a natural progression from the Donation of Constantine. The Donation of Constantine was derived from the Eucharist bestowed of Ptolemy V Epiphany Eucharistos. The Eucharist is a perversion of the symbolic anointment of Horus as governor of Egypt and vicar of the Sun RA and the actual elevation of an Ancient

Egyptian priest as Pharaoh of Egypt. The anointment of Horus is symbolic of the Ennead and Memphite Theology creation stories which are representative of the Earth's orbit of the Sun. The Earth's orbit of the Sun ultimately reveals the power of knowledge especially as it pertains to our environment.

With nature as their ultimate book, teacher and University and by incorporating and embodying nature in their political, governmental and spiritual institutions the Ancient Egyptians were the Ultimate naturalists.

Summary, Enhanced Recapitulation and Conclusion

The creators of civilization established a prism of light that has enlightened the world. From this prism of light enlists a gallery and spectrum of names Africa, Oriental Africa, The Ancient Nile Valley, Kemet, Nubia and Ancient Egypt which in varying nuances and functions helped start civilization throughout the world.

There is a profound reason why Christmas and the New Year are annually used in the same salute. The greeting "Merry Christmas and Happy New Year" literally translates into Happy New Year and Happy New Years.

New Year's Day is a holiday which directly signifies the Solar anniversary; Christmas indirectly denotes the start of the New Year, it is the holiday that was originally celebrated as the birthday of the Sun. The birthday of the Sun equals the start of the Earth's orbit of the Sun which equals the start of the New Year.

Christmas supposedly represents the celebration of Jesus Christ's birthday. The Christ portion of the name Jesus is not a proper name, but a title; the title Christ is derived from the Greek word Christos which in turn came from the word Messias which means anointed one.

To anoint was a practice that was designed to set apart, to make sacred or to declare one holy. Initially this process was applied to any Ancient Egyptian priest or priestess who was selected to ascend from the priesthood to become Pharaoh. In doing so, the Pharaoh was said to take on the characteristics of Horus, who is the representative of the Sun.

Note: *The Melchite Coptic Egyptians first applied the term Christos to Serapis and Ptolemy V, Epiphanes Eucharistos in 196 B.C.E. in order to give honor to Ptolemy V, Epiphanes Eucharistos.*

Every Pharaoh who governed Egypt sat on the throne of Isis (Aset) as the vicar of Horus , who is the universal Ancient Egyptian's deity (who was recognized as the Son of the Sun or the Sun of the Creator).

In like manner, after a council of Coptic Egyptian priests created the god Serapis in the image of Ptolemy I Lagi in 320 B.C.E. by giving this man-made entity the assimilated characteristic of Horus. Every Greek Ptolemy and every Roman Caesar who ruled Egypt, ruled Egypt as the vicar of Serapis. Centuries later in 421 A.B.C.E. the Exterior Coptic Religious community bestowed on the image of Serapis the title Christos or Christo. With the consensus and recognition of both the Melchite Egyptians and the Exterior Coptic Egyptians on Serapis as the Christos, completed the apotheosizing process that converted the image of Serapis into Christos or Christ. See Dr. Walter Williams' The Historical Origin of Christianity.

The resurrection of the Sun occurs during the Vernal Equinox, when the Sun appears to cross the equator transcending from the Southern to the Northern Hemisphere.

The significance of the cross goes far beyond the origin of Christianity. This cross was derived from the swastika, an ancient symbol that reaches back to its origin the ankh. When the cross is used to partition the Moon, it represents the four lunar phases, the New Moon, the Half Moon, the Full Moon and the Old Moon. At the moment the cross is used to dissect the Earth, it designates the four cardinal points, North, South, East and West. The cross, the ankh and the swastika are symbolically one. They represent the Earth's orbit of the Sun and the four GEO/SOLAR OCCURRENCES; when the symbols are used to intersect the Sun, they are representative of the Winter Solstice, Vernal Equinox, the Summer Solstice and the Autumnal Equinox.

Christmas (New Year's Day) now designated as a mass or celebration for Christ is celebrated on December 25th. Epiphany or Little Christ or Little Christmas is celebrated from December 26th through January 6th, which is called the Twelfth night.

Since the Renaissance Era, December 25th has been defined as a holiday that was originally celebrated by "pagans". According to Western sources, this contrived day is allegedly the date that The Coptic Egyptians or pagans celebrated the birth of the Sun and this day later was adopted by Christianity as the birthday of Jesus the Christ.

This is nonsensical, the Ancient Egyptians created astronomy. They

113

based their entire society on the principles that governed the relationship between the Earth, Moon and Sun, the Vernal, Autumnal Equinoxes, Winter and Summer Solstices. Consequently, the Ancient Egyptians would never create a Solar holiday on a non eventful day of December 25th to celebrate the birthday of the Sun when they could denote this day on a date that coincides with a Solar occurrence, thereby stamping the significance of this event with a natural event. As a matter of logic and fact, the recognition of the significance of this natural Solar occurrence was the source, inspiration and motivation for the holiday in the first place.

The Ancient Egyptians celebrated the birthday of the Sun or Horus on the day of the Winter Solstice; based on the current calendar this day would be December 21st or December 22nd. In the Northern Hemisphere, this is the first day of winter and I deem it to be the first day of the New Year. The significance of this day is that in the Northern Hemisphere the Winter Solstice is the shortest day of the year in terms of the time between Sunrise and Sunset. This is also the day that the Sun appears to reach it's lowest point in the atmosphere and starts its ascension in the Southern Hemisphere. For the Ancient Egyptians, this day represented the beginning of winter, the birth of the Sun and the start of the New Year. Even though New Years Day is currently celebrated on January 1st, seven days after Christmas; New Years Day and Christmas are both synonymous with the start of the New Year.

Thanksgiving is not generally thought to be directly associated with Christmas nor is it thought to be linked to the tenets of Christian doctrine; however, upon a closer examination we will find that Thanksgiving is actually a critical element of the Christmas concept. In the United State's Thanksgiving occurs about a month before Christmas. It is given a United States identity by associating it to an element of questionable United States history to preclude it from its' real association. This history states that during one cold winter a group of early American settlers who were unprepared for the harsh American winter, were rescued from certain death by a group of native Americans; these charitable people provided the pilgrims with enough food, clothing and shelter for them to survive the winter. The following year these settlers showed their appreciation from the favors the native Americans bestowed upon them by inviting them to a banquet, this banquet became an annual event and later evolved into the holiday that we know today as Thanksgiving.

However, the true origins of Thanksgiving are not based in U.S.

history. A Thanksgivings Holiday is also celebrated in at least two other countries, Canada and England. The foundation for Thanksgiving goes back to the era of Ptolemy V, Epiphanes Eucharisto and beyond, to the time when the Ancient Egyptians created the Lunar based calendar system. All Ptolemy rulers were offsprings of the original Greek ruler who invaded Egypt in 332 B.C.E. In 196 B.C.E. a council of Melchite Coptic Egyptian Priests and Priestesses in Memphis Egypt created the Rosetta stone and the Eucharist ritual to commemorate the coronation of Ptolemy V. In this celebration Ptolemy V was renamed Ptolemy V Epiphanes Eucharist. The Eucharist was a special honor conducted in the three Serapeum Temples, including the Dionysian, the Serapeum and the Mithream Temples. This honor was designed to thank Ptolemy V for the many favors given by him to the Melchite priest society. It was the first order of service and it expresses complete dedication to Ptolemy V acting as the vicar of Serapis, see The Last Supper. On a much deeper level Thanksgiving is derived from the Lunar based calendar, the name Epiphanes is synonymous with Epact. It is the part of Ptolemy V name which denotes the number 12. The name Eucharisto is that element of Ptolemy V name which denotes the concept of Thanksgiving. The combination of both names equate to a Twelve day Thanksgiving or celebration. This celebration ultimately refers to the 12 extra days beyond the 12 natural months that it takes to complete one year or before the start of the New Year. Therefore Thanksgiving is equivalent to the 11 days before the start of the New Year plus New Year's Day and is a prelude to the New Year.

The Ancient Egyptians based their year on 12 natural months; however, a year based on 12 natural months only has 354 days, 11.25 days short of a Earth year. The concept of Epiphany or "little Christ" was conceived as a means to add these additional 11.25 days to the lunar year to bring the lunar year in line with the Earth year and to further highlight the Winter Solstice (New Year's Day) by celebrating those additional 11.25 days with New Year's Day as the prelude to New Year's Day. The 11.25 days were recognized as 12 days and became symbolic of the twelve natural months of the lunar year. Hence the designation "little Christ", "little Christmas", little year and the Thanksgiving all of which are homogeneous.

Even though the 11.25 days of Epact are accounted for in the Jewish calendar with the addition of an extra month within every three year period and another extra month within a nineteen year period, this period is so critical to Jewish theology and the Jewish calendar that it is also celebrated every year. In Judaism, Epact or The Thanksgiving is celebrated in relationship with the Autumnal Equinox starting with the Jewish holiday Rosh Hashanah and ending 11 days later with the Jewish high holiday Yom Kippur, New Year's Day and Day of Atonement.

In Christianity, twelve natural months and twelve days constitute one Earth year. Subsequently, the twelfth day after the twelfth month represents New Year's Day, the day of the Winter Solstice. New Year's Day personifies both closure and onset or inception, the ending and the beginning. Also the twelfth day combines the old year with the new year because approximately six hours of the old year and eighteen hours of the new year are incorporated within this day.

According to Western academia, the stellar, solar and lunar phases were different and independent periods in which the Ancient Egyptians emphasized the stars, Sun and Moon respectively in their development of educational, spiritual and social institutions. This concept however is a misconception, because the stars and the Moon have little or no importance outside of the Sun and how they relate to the Earth's orbit of the Sun. Therefore, there was never a period or phase in which the Moon or stars were featured without the Sun being the central theme.

Why is it that many religions throughout the world are orientated toward the east? Why is it that Muslims pray toward the East? Is it because their holy land Mecca is located in the East? Why is it that many Christian denominations pray toward the East? Is it because their holy land Jerusalem is located in the East? Or is the reasoning esoteric and using the same rationale that explains why Japan is known as the land of the rising Sun. The Sun rises in the East and is the hidden motif that drives the majority of the world's established historical religions. Most religions from their inceptions are corrupt spin-offs of the Ancient Egyptians Spiritual system. In Oriental Africa or Ancient Egypt, the Sun was highly revered because the Ancient Egyptians understood the controlling influences of the Sun on the Earth's environment.

Because, not all four seasons are completely contained within a calendar year, this condition illuminates the fact that the Gregorian calendar is a politically contrived entity. Under any circumstances it is illogical and unnatural to start the beginning season of a New Year in the previous Year especially when the Earth year completely contains all four Seasons.

The divine rights of kings can be tracked back from the Sun, to the European kings head gear. This golden crown that these king wore with the spiky flare standing up around the crown, is representative of the flaring Sun (Ra) the Creator, which also represents that ring of light that appears around the head of "Jesus the Christ" known as a halo or nimbus. This actually represents the Sun and is a perversion of that ring of light, the Sun disk, which appears on the head of Horus in many depictions of him throughout Egypt.

The Christmas tree, with or without a star at its top, is a representation of the many Ancient Egyptians pyramids found in Nubia and that exist in many European countries with historic ties to the Egyptians during the so called classical Era. These pyramids have a relatively small base, they are tall with a very steep angular profile.

In ancient times and even now, the time of year could be determined naturally by two methods. 1.) By noticing the Moon phase at the start of the year and counting the number of phase cycles since the start of the new year. 2.) By gazing up into the eastern skies right before dawn to notice which zodiacal constellation is in session. The zodiac constellation indicates the month and the Moon phase indicates the relative week and the day within the month. Previously, the Moon was shown to be a critical component in the formulation of a comprehensive time concept.

The powerful natural hidden principles **Epact**, the **Metonic Cycle** and the **Saros Cycle** demonstrate the importance of understanding the Lunar cycle as it pertains to calendar maintenance and the ability to predict Solar Eclipse. When we gain some understanding of the previous mentioned lunar principles we can automatically eliminate the pretend confusion Western scholars have when it comes to the length of the lunar cycle. Is the functional cycle 27.333 days, 29.5 days or 30 days? All of the above principles are based on 29.5 days.

However, the Moon had another important function, to illuminate the skies after Sundown. Currently, it might be hard to see what an important role Moon beams or Moon light played throughout time. However, up until a hundred and fifty years ago the effects of Moon light were obvious. Now modern man has become blind to the conditions of the pre-electric age, when the evening skies were extremely dark, unless the skies were lit up by light coming from the Moon or/and the stars. However, even today it would only take one to travel to a remote region and stay in this location for one natural month to experience the full effects that the natural Moon lighting provides during this period. Second to the Sun, and more than all the other Astronomical bodies combined, the Moon in varying degrees provided natural lighting after dark that has helped to extend the practical work day.

Although a great deal of effort has been taken to conceal the role that the Sun has played in the establishment of Western Society and institutions, today the Sun is worshipped overtly at least once a week on the day that is dedicated to it, Sun Day. Sunday literally means "Day of the Sun" It is observed by most Christian denominations as the Lord's Day (Christ) or day of worship. In all of its aspect, whether it was the original Ancient Egyptians version, or the perverted Christian version, the Christ concept ultimately reverts back to the Sun, the essence and life.

1) Christ (perverted) = Serapis

2) Serapis (perverted) = Horus

3) Horus = Sun

4) Sun = Creation and the Creator

With the Sun as the object and central theme of Ancient Egypt's, educational, spiritual and political institutions through emblems, and parables became the conduits of critical solar knowledge. This information helps to define and predict natural events which are the prelude to settled living: the establishment of villages, towns and cities are the forerunners to high civilization.

Historically, and today, the "secrets" of the Sun can ultimately be translated as the secrets of the Son relating to "Christ" and Christianity in particular, and Islam and Judaism in general. The Secrets of the Sun is the revelation of the solar principles symbolized by the world's educational, political and spiritual institutions as the foundation for civilization. The natural year and calendar is at the core of this awakening. Religions are not spiritually inspired nor are they the inspiration of some mythical god; originally, Western religions are derived directly from the Ancient Egyptians spiritual systems and were the metaphor for the Earth's annual orbit of the Sun. Moreover, now they are also the principle means to disseminate the myth of white supremacy. The purpose of Western culture is to promote the myth of white supremacy. However, before the myth of white supremacy can be promoted, Western academia by way of the Greeks gave themselves credit for most, if not all, of the collective knowledge of the world. The whole continent of Africa was given an inferiority label and made void of any redeemable values. Prior to this action, Ancient Egypt was disassociated from the rest of Africa. It is impossible to physically and culturally remove Ancient Egypt from the continent of Africa. Nevertheless, an all out attempt has been made to psychologically remove Egypt from Africa by culturally, economically and politically associating Egypt with the politically created region known today as the Middle East.

Western culture has falsely convinced the world of the inferiority of African people. Subconsciously, many Africans convinced of and ashamed by their supposed inferiority have gravitated to those things that they think will give them more validation and will make them more respectable and acceptable to the rest of the world. Ironically, Western institutions are the source of these myths, lies and ultimately most of the problems of the descendants of African people.

Politically, and spiritually, Western religions pose the greatest barrier to the liberation of the African mind, being personified with European characters and loaded with Western philosophies. After centuries of development Western religions were designed to suppress the African origin of civilization, while establishing the myth of white supremacy. The nature of Western religions is to pacify the masses and to subjugate the world with the image of a European man as the Creator and/or the SON OF GOD.

In an attempt to further its yoke of deception Western academia has effectively diverted both attention and critical analysis from the Gregorian and Jewish Calendars by highlighting the undeciphered "Ancient Egyptian calendar" as the key source for the interpretation of the mysteries of Antiquity. However, the study of natural cycles and Western calendars are two of the most important keys to understanding the true purpose of Western religions and the development of civilization. Besides the hundreds, perhaps thousands, of native cultures who observe the Moon to establish time, in the Americas, Asia and Africa, today the Lunar based calendar is practiced overtly by at least two politically powerful groups of people: 1.) The people of China 2.) The people who practice the religion known as Judaism.

Covertly, however the Western world maintains both a present and historic connection with the Lunar based calendar by way of the Passover/ Easter interface (Holidays). This interface allows the natural attributes of both the perverted Jewish and Gregorian calendars to be extracted and combined to produce a totally nature based calendar founded on Lunar months(what is today deemed The Jewish calendar) with a 365.25 day year (The Gregorian calendar).

Every year the four GEO/SOLAR OCCURRENCES pass with little or no fanfare. This belies the vital role these occurrences play in defining the year and the seasons, and subsequently conceals the powerful role they played in the development of the world's major spiritual, political and educational institutions. The Ancient Egyptian recognized the importance of the four GEO/SOLAR OCCURRENCES winter, spring, summer, and autumn to the point they highlighted and encoded their perspective start date. However, the European scholar community has systematically contaminated and obscured these functions. Today Christmas and New Year's Day together are the corrupted mimesis for the December Solstice and in like manner Easter and Passover are the perverted mimesis for the March Equinox.

The Lunar and Zodiac calendars were used to gauge Earth's advancement into its orbit and the year. The four GEO/SOLAR OCCURRENCES were divided and distributed into the Gregorian and Jewish calendars. Later, the attributes of these occurrences were hidden in Christianity, Islam and Judaism, the three major Western religions, in the form of religious holy days.

The creation of the time concept was the most fundamental and powerful event in the development of civilization. The Sun, the Moon and the Earth are, in the Ancient Egyptians Divine triad or Trilogy time concept, the three critical elements in the establishment of time as symbolized in the Ennead: the father (The Sun), the Sun (the Son the Moon), and the Holy Cow (the Mother Earth).

The three principal pyramids of Giza also represent this time trilogy and should henceforth be designated as the Pyramid of the Sun, the Pyramid of Earth and the Pyramid of the Moon.

The consequence of the Earth's orbit of the Sun dictates Earth's environment. The study of natural cycles, the development of a concept of time, and the creation of the calendar all revolve around understanding and reckoning with the changes that are evoked by the Earth's annual journey around the Sun.

The Winter Solstice (December Solstice), Vernal Equinox (March Equinox), Summer Solstice (June Solstice) and the Autumnal Equinox (September Equinox), the four GEO/SOLAR OCCURRENCES are natural holidays and are the only days worthy of universal respect. Globally, these sacred days should be recognized as cardinal holidays because they are the precursors to the changes in the Earth's environment and they are the secret principle behind the major Western and world religions and, Western society's ultimate controlling force.

MUSEUM OF ANTIQUITY, CAIRO EGYPT; KING TUTANKHAMUN FUNERAL MASK   (A)

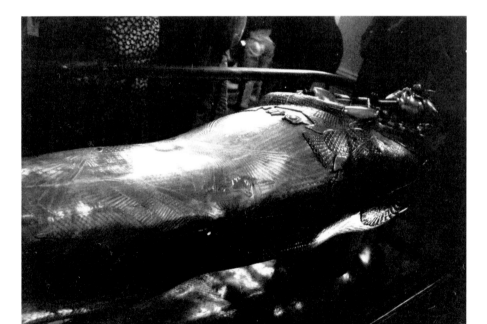

KING TUTANKHAMUN COFFIN   (B)

King Tutankhamun coffin (A)

Stone figures of Akhenaten and Family (B)

THE THREE PYRAMIDS AT GIZA, PYRAMID OF THE SUN, EARTH AND MOON (A)

THE PYRAMID OF THE EARTH AND THE PYRAMID OF THE SUN (B)

THE GREAT SPHINX OF GIZA (A)

THE GREAT PYRAMID OR THE PYRAMID OF THE SUN (B)

THE STEP PYRAMID AT SAQQARA (A)

THE MAIN TEMPLE AT SAQQARA (B)

INSIDE THE MAIN TEMPLE AT SAQQARA (A)

A MUD BUILDING COMPLEX (B)

THE VALLEY OF THE KINGS; THE MORTUARY TEMPLE OF HATSHEPSUT (A)

A POWERFUL IMAGE OF HATHOR AND THE PHARAOH (B)

THE COLOSSALS OF MEMNON (A)

THE TEMPLE OF HORUS; INSIDE THE OUTER TEMPLE WALLS (B)

THE AUTHOR STANDING NEXT TO HORUS AS THE HAWK IN FRONT OF THE INNER   (A)
TEMPLE WALLS

THE BOAT THAT SAILS THROUGH THE UNDERWORLD EVERY NIGHT   (B)

THE TEMPLE OF HORUS (A)

THE GRAND ENTRANCE OF THE KARNAK TEMPLE; THE AVENUE OF THE SPHINX (B)

THE DOUBLE ROLL OF HUGE TEMPLE COLUMNS (A)

THE GIGANTIC SEATED TEMPLE AT ABU SIMBEL (B)

INSIDE THE GIGANTIC SEATED TEMPLE (A)

A COLUMN INSIDE THE LARGE STANDING TEMPLE (B)

THE THREE SMALLER PYRAMIDS THAT ACCOMPANY THE PYRAMID OF THE MOON.   (A)

THE THREE SMALL PYRAMIDS AND TEMPLE OUTSIDE THE GREAT PYRAMID OF THE SUN (B)

THE COLUMNS AT LUXOR (A)

THE OBELISK AND COLUMNS AT KARNAK (B)

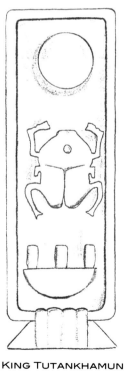

KING TUTANKHAMUN
CARTOUCHE (C)

BOYS WAVING IN THE MARKETPLACE (A)

YOUNG MEN WAITING TO RECEIVE THEIR CARGO (B)

WOMAN ON THE HIGH BANK DRAWING WATER FROM THE NILE   (A)

MEN REBUILDING A MUD BRICK HOUSE NEAR THE NILE   (B)

CHILDREN PLAYING AND BATHING IN THE NILE (A)

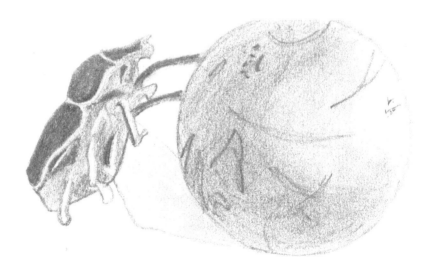

DUNG BEETLE ROLLING DUNG,
SYMBOLIC OF THE SUN MOVING ACROSS THE SKY (B)

Summary

ANCIENT EGYPT AND THE SECRETS OF THE SUN

In conclusion, Book I, and Book II are the preface and preamble to Book III.

Book I, Western Philosophy: Facts or Theories and Lies

Book I is designed to encourage the reader to not only question, but to challenge the unquestionable status that Western academia has established for itself as the ultimate authority of what's wrong or right or what's trivial or important.

Western academia uses a closed documentation system to support their claims or contentions. This forces anyone who goes through it's educational system to use sources that are only endorsed by this system. As a result students are trained to think only within the boundaries that these sources allow. At this point the students thinking is practically enslaved by this powerful paradigm.

By listing academic principles and theories that the author believes defy logic and common sense, but have long been accepted principles, the author attempts to broaden the views and thinking of the reader by analyzing, highlighting and revealing the strong conflicts that exist between these theories and their practices. When considering the fact that Western academia is not the ultimate authority, but should be questioned at every level, because many of the principles and contentions of Western academia are based on lies, theories and half-truths, it is the desire of the author that when this is made clear to the world, this book will be viewed as a much more serious challenger of Western academia in general and even an greater challenger to the misinformation intentionally assigned to the Ancient Egyptians and their descendants.

Book II,   Africa and African Misunderstood

Book II, emphasizes, highlights and reconnects Egypt with the rest of the African continent. The people of Sub-Saharan Africa have been systematically disconnected with Egypt in an attempt to dissolve their cultural, racial and historical oneness, as if they were and are diametrically opposed. In surveying a number of books based on the Ancient Egyptians, not one of these books had a map of Egypt which depicts Egypt within the continent of Africa, rather they display maps of Egypt proper or maps of northeastern Africa. Book II, also reveals the many major contributions Africans have made to the world in terms of social development, music, the arts, steel making and medicine.

Book III,   Ancient Egypt = The Sun (RA), Time, Spirituality and a High Civilization

Book III, reveals Ancient Egypt as the place where the Concept of Time was established, resulting in the development of civilization and High civilization.

Ancient and Modern Egypt exist in the Northeastern regions of the African Continent. The Ancient Egyptians were an African People who left tens of thousands of monuments and images behind to remind their descendants and the rest of the world of their true identity.

All knowledge emanates from nature. The Ancient Egyptians were the first and most prolific students of nature. That which has become esoteric today, is that nature, not perverted Western education institutions, is the ultimate teacher and nature not perverted Western institutions is the ultimate source of knowledge. From beginning to end of the Ancient Egyptians civilization the Sun was their principal and most powerful motif. Through their keen observation of the environment, in conjunction with daily observance of the Sun, the Sun along with the Earth and Moon became the Ancient Egyptian astronomical clock and calendar.   The Ancient Egyptians orientated themselves to the Sun; cyclical rhythms were observed, noted and encoded as the foundation of their knowledge base. This critical information became sacred and was set aside. With the recognitions of The Geo/Solar occurrences (The December Solstice, The March Equinox, The June Solstice and The September Equinox) brought predictability into their environment through the Earth's advancement into its cyclical orbit of the Sun. Today this critical information is the foundation for Western religions and this foundation establishes Western religions most important and powerful holidays.

Picture writing was created to allow this information to be stored and formatted into the Ancient Egyptians creation stories, in practice the Ancient Egyptian creation stories became their constitution.

The European table of nations looks to the Greeks as their progenitor and founder.

Not only can the people of the African continent look to the Ancient Egyptians as their progenitor. The whole Ancient and modern world should look to the Ancient Egyptian as the ultimate creators of civilization and of high civilization.

Finally, even though the Western world seems to support the year based on the Gregorian calendar, the true purpose of the Easter/Passover interface or holidays is to maintain a natural year based on 365.25 days with 12 natural months (months based on the Lunar cycle 29.5 day) plus 11.25 days. The real natural year and calendar.

With the reordering and re-shuttering of what's true, important and trivial, or who did what, when and where, reemerges the African continent and its original people as the direct descendants of the Ancient Egyptians, and as the main contributor and giver of civilization to the world.

Pictures, Graphs and Illustrations Index

About the Author

Jerry Parker was born in Leland Mississippi in 1952. He was the ninth child out of ten children. He advanced to the first grade before his family moved in 1959, to the westside of Chicago.

While living on the westside of Chicago, he attended several elementary schools including Lawson, Trailor School in Douglas Park , Lathrup and Hess Upper Grade Center. Before the 8th grade he and his family moved to the southside of Chicago, where he attended Cook elementary school for one year.

Before he attended Calumet High School, Calumet's High School band director went to Cook and other surrounding schools to recruit new band members. As a result Jerry decided to go to Calumet High School, study the trumpet and joined the beginners band, two years later he joined the school's Marching and Concert Band. Although he had no apparent athletic skills, after seeing a former Cook school classmate on stage as a member of the cross country and track teams, he decided to join those teams as well.

Jerry Parker attended Calumet High School from 1967 1971. In 9th grade he was mistakenly assigned to the World Geography class. During this time Calumet was transitioning from a White majority student population to a school with a majority Black student population. This was occurring during the time of Black Power or Black conscience era.

The teacher of his World Geography class was a young White woman. Ironically being from the south, this class was his first exposure to the deadly politics of race.

Jerry learned about the current status of race relations in South Africa, where all rights were stolen from the original African inhabitants. They were then assigned to homelands, regions mostly comprised of barren deserts to try to make a living as tribal farmers. The Europeans, minorities living in South Africa at that time, created a class system concentrating and saving all the real political and economic power for themselves. Assigning the native Africans and the mixed peoples a menial role. This injustice lit a spark.

During this time Jerry was enrolled in several Black History courses. Also the schools English department featured many Black literary

144

giants from that era. It was here that his understanding and knowledge expanded to what was happening in America. He recognized how similar the circumstances where to those happening in South Africa. He learned of the brutality, oppression, tricks, including the flood of drugs, alcohol and firearms in Black communities. He noticed in his own community, groups of people hanging around liquor stores waiting for them to open their doors early in the morning. During this time he made a pledge to never drink, smoke or use drugs. Jerry recognized at an early age that the purpose of his pledge was to try to lower the number of his people who were being tricked into submission and not given a fighting chance to counter the yoke of oppression placed on his people. But what was even worse in his eyes, was the effect that drugs had on the people and how many amongst his ranks had become addicts. He realized that Western society was trying to make the Black community ineffective to combat the assault on the humanity of African people. To the point that Western society tried to portray as proof skewed examples of a race of born criminals, subhumans, not worthy of life and project this manipulated viewpoint to the world as fact through broadcasting media and political leaders that parroted these views. The fire of knowledge and consciousness had been ignited in him.

In 1971 Jerry Parker received a band scholarship from Texas Southern University (a HBCU), where he received a Bachelors of Music Education (All level, instrumental). Being a new student with an instrumental major and band scholarship made being a member of the marching band and concert band mandatory. It was his band instructor that talked him into joining the Jazz band as well. To receive a bachelors at Texas Southern Music Education program required a grueling 176 course hours, broken down into 3 major disciplines, Music, Education and Psychology. In Jerry's opinion, the Ocean of Soul Marching Band was the greatest marching band ever.

It has been stated that marching bands at historically Black colleges and universities practiced more than many of the school's football teams. Jerry's standard day of practice in those days, would include a full day of regular college courses, then band practice would start after dinner. This would include learning new popular music for the week, learning dance routines, then putting it all together by the end of the week. Being a member of such a respected marching band had many honors and perks associated with it, including performing in:

The Astrodome in Houston,
Dallas Stadium,
The Superdome in New Orleans,
The Mardi Gras Parade in New Orleans
The University of Hawaii

His band played in all of the SWAC cities including Jackson Mississippi, the home of the great Walter Payton, a future NFL legend. In Jerry's first year at Texas Southern University Jazz Band, the band won the Southwest Regional College Jazz Festival. This festival was part of the four regionals contest that culminated with the ultimate honor of all four performing at the Kennedy Center for performing arts in Washington D.C. The Texas Southern Jazz Band created a jazz album based on this triumphant performance. Jerry is still eternally grateful to the Director of Bands and his assistants for allowing him to be part of such a dynamic musical organization.

During his time at Texas Southern he met a fellow Mississpian, from Mount Byu, who majored in Electronics. This fellow student talked about this relatively new field of computer programming, he claimed that one mistake entering a computer command would cause a malfunction. He would brag these abilities required more than average brain skills and explained that is why he was an Honor student. Jerry interpreted these boasts as a personal challenge. Already with a full schedule, Jerry decided to use his 'free' time to take classes in FORTRAN programming. He enjoyed the classes so much he decided to spend all of his 'extra' time in the computer center experimenting with writing different types of computer applications to solve business, math and logical problems. Later he was awarded a part time job at the IBM data center working with an original IBM 1401. Even though he did not officially change his major, it was at this point he changed his focus on music theory to computer logic. From wanting to be a music teacher and composer to being a computer programmer.

To his surprise, many of his family members travelled to Houston and proudly celebrated with Jerry Parker, the college graduate.

After graduating Jerry and his family headed back to Chicago. Jerry looked for jobs in both the educational and computer fields. During this time he had come across two books that became his favorites,

The Autobiography of Malcolm X and Malcolm X on Afro American History. These books rekindled the fire that burned in him about the African history and Black studies.

In 1977 Jerry found a job in the computer field. During that same year he attended Loop College in Chicago to learn new computer languages that being implemented at his new job. It was during this time a very close family member showed him an article in the newspaper about a book titled THEY CAME BEFORE COLUMBUS, by Ivan Van Sertima. This book relit the flame in his heart about African History. He would re-read this book from cover to cover. This book revealed to him information not mentioned in mainstream history books, like the presence of Ancient Egyptians and Western Africans in the Americas as builders and promoters of high civilizations. (In Mexico, Central America and Ancient American Indian mounts along the Mississippi river, in North America hundreds of years before Christopher Columbus.) The Atlantic Ocean drift routes were the "highways" that brought thousands of boats and vessels from Africa to America landing in the Gulf of Mexico in an area now called Olmec. Jerry later met Ivan Van Sertima at a lecture at the UICC campus. This initiated his joining of a study and research group of Ancient History. That group then stimulated two trips to Egypt. One trip he went alone in 1985 and the second trip in 1992 with a study group. In Egypt Jerry was able to look upon the ancient ruins with his own eyes, which led him to more independent in depth African and Ancient Egyptian studies. Jerry absorbed so much information, understanding and knowledge during these trips and discovered so much about the relationships of between earth and the sun according to Africa's ancients, that he was compelled to write this book and share this knowledge with his people and all who honor truth over manipulation.

Bibliography

1. NATURE, A careful observation and analysis of the daily movement of the Sun and the Moon as it relates to the daily changes in the Earth's environment. *

2. Ancient Egypt's Sites and monuments. Eyewitness to and critical analysis of, the monuments of Ancient Egypt: The pyramids, the temples, Obelisks and Subterranean burial chambers in their original and natural environment. **

3. The Historical Origin of Christianity, Dr. Walter Williams (Maathian Press, Inc., Chicago, IL 1992).

4. Malcolm X on Afro-American History, Betty Shabazz and Pathfinder Press (Pathfinder Press, New York, NY 1970).

5. They Came Before Columbus, Ivan Van Sertima (Random House, New York, NY 1976).

6. The African Origin of Christianity, John G. Jackson, (L. & P. Enterprises, Chicago, IL 1976).

7. I Sought My Brother : An Afro-American Reunion, S. Allen Counter and David L. Evans (The Massachusetts Institute of Technology, 1981).

8. The African Origin Of Civilization Myth Or Reality, Cheikh Anta Diop, (Lawrence Hill Books, Chicago, IL 1974).

9. Stolen Legacy, George G.M. James, (Julian Richardson, 1976).

10. The Destruction of Black Civilization, Chancelor Williams, (Third World Press, Chicago, IL . 1976).

11. Introduction to African Civilization, John G. Jackson (Citadel Press, Secaucus, NJ, 1970).

12. Atlas of Ancient Egypt, John Baines and Jaromir Malek, (Facts on File Publications, New York, N.Y. 10019, 1980).

13. Nile Valley Contributions To Civilization Anthony Browder, (The Institute of Karmic Guidance, Washington, D.C. 1992).

14. African Religions and Philosophy, John S. Mbiti, (Anchor Books Doubleday & Company, Inc., Garden City, N.Y. 1969)

15. The World and Africa, W.E.B. Du Bois (International Publishers Co., Inc. 1946, 1947).

16. The African Genius, Basil Davidson, (Atlantic-Little, Brown Books, U.S.A.1969).

17. Kingship and the Gods, Henri Frankfort (University of Chicago Press, Chicago IL 1948).

18. The Gods And Symbols of Ancient Egypt, Manfred Lurker, (Thames and Hudson Inc., 500 Fifth Avenue, New York, N.Y. 1982).

19. Field Enterprises Educational Corporation. The World Book Encyclopedia (Field Enterprises Educational Corporation, Chicago IL 1973).

20. Abu Simbel - Ghizeh Guide Book/Manual,Y.A.A. ben-Jochannan's , (Yosef A. A. ben-Jochannan, New York, N.Y. 1986).

21. A History of Egypt, James Henry Breasted, (Charles Scribner's Sons., New York, N.Y. 1937).

22. Shore, D. Steel-Making in Ancient Africa. Blacks in Science, Ancient and Modern, I. Van Sertima, New Brunswick: Transaction Books, 1983, pp.157-162.

23. Sex and Race, Volume 1, 2, & 3, J.A. Rogers, (Helga M. Rogers St. Petersburg, Florida 33711, 1967)

Note: (*) The source of all knowledge emanates from nature. It is time for African scholars to circumvent perverted Western sources and go back to the real source of knowledge, Nature and the Earth's annual orbit of the Sun!

Note: (**) With logic, a fresh perspective devoid of Western philosophy and misleading paradigms the TRUTH CAN BE OBTAINED.

NOTES

NOTES

NOTES

NOTES

ANCIENT EGYPT AND THE SECRETS OF THE SUN

BY JERRY PARKER
PARKER.JERRY@COMCAST.NET

AVAILABLE AT BOOK STORES
OR IT CAN BE ORDERED BY FILLING OUT THE
FOLLOWING FORM AND WITH
YOUR CHECK OR MONEY ORDER

PRICE PER COPY $24.00

FOR 1 COPY... $24.00

FOR 2 COPIES..$48.00

FOR 3 COPIES.. $72.00

OR_____COPIES X $24.00   =   SUBTOTAL_____

PLUS: SHIPPING/HANDLING (6.00) PER 1ST BOOK;
(3.00) PER ADDITIONAL BOOK_____

TOTAL_____

MAKE CHECK PAYABLE TO
JERRY PARKER
P.O. BOX 377640
CHICAGO, ILLINOIS 60637-7940

NAME_____

STREET ADDRESS_____

_____

CITY, STATE, ZIP_____

ALLOW FOUR WEEKS FOR DELIVERY